Deleuze and Lola Montès

FILM THEORY IN PRACTICE

Series Editor: Todd McGowan

Deleuze and Lola Montès

RICHARD RUSHTON

BLOOMSBURY ACADEMIC

NEW YORK · LONDON · OXFORD · NEW DELHI · SYDNEY

BLOOMSBURY ACADEMIC
Bloomsbury Publishing Inc
1385 Broadway, New York, NY 10018, USA

BLOOMSBURY, BLOOMSBURY ACADEMIC and the Diana logo are trademarks of
Bloomsbury Publishing Plc

First published in the United States of America 2021

Cover design: Eleanor Rose
Cover image © Vince Cavataio/Getty Images

Library of Congress Cataloging-in-Publication Data

Names: Rushton, Richard, author.
Title: Deleuze and Lola Montès / Richard Rushton.
Description: New York: Bloomsbury Academic, 2020. | Series: Film theory in practice |
Includes bibliographical references and index.
Identifiers: LCCN 2020029963 (print) | LCCN 2020029964 (ebook) |
ISBN 9781501345753 (paperback) | ISBN 9781501345760 (hardback) |
ISBN 9781501345784 (epub) | ISBN 9781501345777 (pdf)
Subjects: LCSH: Deleuze, Gilles, 1925-1995. | Lola Montès (Motion picture)
Classification: LCC B2430.D454 .R87 2020 (print) | LCC B2430.D454 (ebook) |
DDC 194–dc23
LC record available at https://lccn.loc.gov/2020029963
LC ebook record available at https://lccn.loc.gov/2020029964

ISBN: HB: 978-1-5013-4576-0
PB: 978-1-5013-4575-3
ePDF: 978-1-5013-4577-7
eBook: 978-1-5013-4578-4

Typeset by Deanta Global Publishing Services, Chennai, India
Printed and bound in the United States of America

To find out more about our authors and books visit www.bloomsbury.com
and sign up for our newsletters.

CONTENTS

ACKNOWLEDGMENTS

Many thanks to colleagues at Lancaster University, especially those who turned out for a Film Club evening some years ago where I presented some ideas on *Lola Montès* just as I was beginning this project. Many thanks to Hyeyoung Maeng for organizing that event and also for being such an excellent Deleuze scholar (and artist). Many thanks, too, must go to the late Beth Harland who had the idea for the Film Club in the first place. Her death came much too soon, and I miss her greatly. Many thanks to my Deleuzian friends—it is far too long since I have seen all of you: David Martin-Jones, Felicity Colman, Will Brown, Anna Powell, Damian Sutton, Bill Marshall, David Fleming, Patricia Pisters, Craig Lundy, Lisa Trahair, Joe Hughes, Ronald Bogue, Michael Goddard, David Deamer, David Rodowick (and, with dismay, many others I will no doubt have forgotten to mention). Warm thanks to Andrew Klevan for some stimulating conversations on Ophuls last summer. And a special thanks to Ian Buchanan for having been such an outstanding scholar and supportive friend for many years.

At Bloomsbury I must thank Katie Gallof for handling many of the organizational details of the book-writing process and Erin Duffy for overseeing a good deal of project's production. Thanks also must go to Todd McGowan as series editor, firstly for having had such an original and brilliant idea for the series and secondly for supporting my contribution.

A very final thanks to Miss Silvia who has once again seen me through thick and thin.

ABBREVIATIONS

Works by Gilles Deleuze:

C1:   *Cinema 1: The Movement-Image*, trans. Hugh Tomlinson and Barbara Habberjam, London: Athlone, 1986.

C2:   *Cinema 2: The Time-Image*, trans. Hugh Tomlinson and Robert Galeta, London: Athlone, 1989.

Works by Henri Bergson:

MM: *Matter and Memory*, trans. N. M Paul and W. S. Palmer, New York: Zone Books, 1996.

CE: *Creative Evolution*, trans. Arthur Mitchell, New York: Henry Holt, 1911.

CHAPTER 1

Deleuze's Cinema
Movement, Time,
Memory, and Subjectivity

A Philosopher Goes to the Movies

Gilles Deleuze wrote two books on cinema, *Cinema 1: The Movement-Image* in 1983 and *Cinema 2: The Time-Image* in 1985. These books offered a remarkable account of cinema history and theory, all informed not only by Deleuze's many years of writing philosophy but also by his love of cinema. He offered conceptions of cinema that were original and provocative, and which went against the grain of the cinema scholarship of the period.

We might first of all ask, what does Deleuze mean by the movement-image and the time-image? These formulations were daring. They challenged the reigning film theory orthodoxies of the 1970s and 1980s. Then, much film theory concentrated on the various ways that cinema, especially mainstream cinema, was seen to be illusory, escapist, or deceptive. Theories advocated by the likes of Jean-Louis Baudry's formulations on the "ideological" nature of the cinema apparatus, or Guy Debord's critique of the "society of the spectacle," and along with it Theodor Adorno's contention that entertainment industries like cinema were forms of "mass deception," all grounded their arguments on the fundamental belief that films and cinema are typically fraudulent, fake, and inauthentic.[1] Against what they saw as being a cinema of deception, these theorists hoped there would emerge a true cinema that would eschew illusion and deception.

Deleuze rejects this distinction between a false cinema and a supposedly true cinema. Far from being critical of cinema as a form of deception, Deleuze can instead be seen as a true lover of cinema. "The cinema is always as perfect as it can be," he wrote in the preface to the English translation of *Cinema 1* (*C1*, x). This means that Deleuze's *Cinema* books set out on a trajectory that is rather different from what had usually been expected of a book of film studies, certainly during the period when the books were written. Deleuze's aim in his writings on cinema is therefore one that eschews any attempt to distinguish between a true cinema and a false cinema, or between good films and bad ones. Rather, his aim is to develop a system of classification of the different types and modes of cinema that existed up until the period when he wrote these two books.

So what are the movement-image and the time-image then? Generally speaking, the movement-image refers to modes and techniques developed in cinema and filmmaking up to the Second World War, while the time-image denotes new techniques that emerged after the Second World War. This definition is very general, however, so that modes associated with the movement-image survived well after the Second World War and, indeed, techniques related to the movement-image remain dominant in cinema today. Likewise, Deleuze claims that aspects of the time-image were always implicit in the movement-image and that some films displayed time-image attributes well before the Second World War, such as films by Carl Theodor Dreyer, Yasujiro Ozu, as well as Max Ophuls, whose works we will come across throughout this book.

What exactly does Deleuze mean by calling these modes the movement-image and the time-image? First of all, as might be expected, movement is crucial for the movement-image, while time is paramount for the time-image. Deleuze means somewhat more than this, however. What is truly remarkable about the movement-image, Deleuze claims, is that it includes movement in the image. This might not initially sound like a particularly revelatory point to make, but given that in the late nineteenth and early twentieth centuries moving images were a genuine innovation—never before in human history had this kind of moving image been produced—Deleuze wants to emphasize that the invention of movement in images was an extraordinary one. Even given the ubiquity of moving images today, there can be little doubt that the invention of moving images was an astonishing one for human history.

Deleuze therefore goes to great lengths to point out that for moving images of the cinema, movement is inside the image; movement is part of the image. In arguing this point, he is countering a classical conception of what cinematographic images are. We know that the process of cinema projection—in the analogue era and also in the digital age—is one in which a series of still images is projected at such a rapid rate (twenty-four frames per second) that viewers of those images perceive them as being in movement. Thus, a standard account of cinema will claim that in reality cinema's images are static: they do not move. The only reason they appear to move is because our perceptual faculties are tricked into seeing movement where in reality there is no such thing. From this perspective, therefore, movement is not part of the image but is merely added to the image, almost as a kind of afterthought. We might also see this as being one of the ways that cinema itself has often been thought to be illusory or deceptive: it does not really give us moving images; rather, we are tricked into seeing movement where there is none. Deleuze rejects such arguments. He declares instead that, even if still images are projected, we do not perceive stillness. We perceive moving images. In other words, what the cinema gives us is a movement-image: images that move and movement that is part of the image. This is why Deleuze calls them movement-images.

If movement is essential to the movement-image, then what is a time-image? I have suggested that the distinction between the movement-image and the time-image is a historical one, and to some extent this is true. But the distinction is much more of a conceptual than historical one. The movement-image designates one way of accounting for what occurs in films, and by association, it also accounts for a certain way of understanding the "real world" too. That way of accounting for things is by way of movement. The time-image then provides a different way of accounting for what occurs in films—and in the "real world" too—in terms of time rather than in terms of movement. Films of the time-image do not prioritize movement, as films of the movement-image do. In many ways the experience of time is one of memory for Deleuze. Time is a matter of the ways that our memories of the past influence our conceptions of the present and our premonitions of the future. As we will see throughout this book, memory is indeed central for films of the time-image. Because film offers ways of capturing images of the present which, as soon as they are photographed, become images of the past, then film offers unique ways of conceiving of the relationship between the past and the present. Deleuze considers that a range of films which emerged after the Second World War took certain aspects of memory as a theme—the "flashback," for example, became a staple of Hollywood cinema during the 1940s.[2] It is therefore films like this, which deal with memory to a large extent and with the relationship between the past and the present, that come to define what is specific to films of the time-image. In what follows I shall detail some aspects of the movement-image and the time-image with reference to a couple of films directed by Max Ophuls.

On Max Ophuls

Max Ophuls was born in Germany in 1902. As a young man in Germany he worked in theater before moving into film direction. Ophuls was Jewish, so after the Nazi Party came to power in 1933, he fled to France, while also spending some time working in Holland and Italy. He made several films in France before then moving to Hollywood during the Second World War. He struggled to find work during the war years in Hollywood, before making a series of distinctive films, none of which was especially successful, though *Letter from an Unknown Woman* (1948) is today regarded as one of the great Hollywood melodramas. In what follows, I engage substantially with *Letter*. Ophuls returned to France in 1950 where he made some of his most highly acclaimed films, including *Lola Montès*. *Lola Montès* (1955) was the last film directed by Ophuls. He died in 1957.

In *Cinema 2*, Deleuze describes *Lola Montès* in terms of flashbacks and multilayered relationships between the past and present (C2, 84). For Deleuze, the film provides a fine example of the time-image. Flashbacks, memories, and relationships between the past and the present are central to many of Ophuls's films, including those made in Hollywood, such as *Letter from an Unknown Woman* or *The Reckless Moment* (1949), or those made elsewhere such as *La Ronde* (France, 1950), or *La signora di tutti* (Italy, 1934). What is very interesting about Ophuls's films overall is that they very often foreground relationships between the past and the present. Yet they do so in varying ways. Often such films will be movement-image films, while at other times they will be time-image films. Thus, some of Ophuls's films prioritize the movement-image, while others place emphasis on the time-image.

How is this so? For those films like *La signora di tutti* (usually translated as *Everybody's Lady*) which offer movement-images rather than time-images, the flashbacks to the past are designed so as *to fix the past in such a way that it will not be subject to change*. Therefore, the task of *La signora di tutti* is to definitively place the past *in the past*, so that what is happening now, in the present, can be clearly distinguished from the past. It is the act of "placing the past in the past" that makes it an example of the movement-image. Let's explore this in a little more detail. What is this film about? Set in Milan and made in 1934, *La signora di tutti* focuses on the life of Gaby Doriot (Isa Miranda). In the film's opening scenes, Gaby is presented to us as a famous film actress who has just signed a lucrative new contract with a movie studio. However, she has just been discovered in her bathroom badly wounded: it is a suicide attempt. She is immediately taken to a hospital and placed under general anesthetic. As she falls under the effect of the anesthetizing gas, the film's images dissolve and we are then treated to a range of flashback episodes that tell the story of Gaby's life.

These episodes unfold in chronological order, beginning with scenes of Gaby's expulsion from school, then moving on to her meeting Roberto Nanni (Friedrich Benfer), thence to her love affair with Roberto's father, Leonardo (Memo Benassi). As the film brings us toward the present, it is revealed that Roberto was, in fact, Gaby's true love, and that it had been a mistake for her to have fallen for Leonardo. To make matters worse, Roberto has married Gaby's sister, Anna (Nelly Corradi), and they are happily married with a child. At the very end of the film, we return to the present. Gaby's suicide attempt has been successful, the surgeons were unable to save her, and she has died.

The film shows us the key attributes of the movement-image. The overall shape of *La signora di tutti* unfolds in the following way: a character in the present, Gaby Doriot, tries to remember the past so she can "put the past in order," so she can discover from the perspective of the present how the past has led to the present. And it was, as both she and we discover, her decision to choose the wrong man that has led to the present situation in which she has attempted suicide: she had an affair with Leonardo when she now realizes she should have married Leonardo's son, Roberto. In this way, the task of the film's narrative is to secure the timeline between past and present, and therefore to explain how and why the past has caused the present situation of Gaby's suicide attempt.

The Movement-Image:
Time as Measurement

As I have claimed, the film is an example of a movement-image. And yet, doesn't this film show us what time is? Isn't this film about relationships between the past, present, and future? If this is so, then why is *La signora di tutti* an example of a movement-image? To complete the timeline of *La signora*, what happened in the past and present leads to the consequence that, in the future, Gaby will no longer be alive: her suicide attempt is successful. But, again, if this is how time seems to work, why is *La signora* an example of a movement-image? Deleuze argues, in ways that will be expanded upon throughout this book, that the movement-image provides one way of conceiving of time. In fact, this way of understanding time—as a timeline in which events and actions are fixed into moments of the past that lead to effects in the present and which then, in turn, will cause certain events and actions to then occur in the future—this way of understanding how time works is not, for Deleuze, a way of conceiving of how time really works. The movement-image does not give us an accurate way of understanding what time is. Rather, Deleuze claims that conceiving of time in terms of a past-present-future pattern in which the past, the present, and the future are clearly separated, is a way of presenting time in terms of measurement. For Deleuze, *time as such cannot be measured*. This is one of the major points he adapts from French philosopher Henri Bergson (1859–1941).

Films of the movement-image therefore present time in terms of the ways that time can be measured—"clock time," as it were. If time is measured then it becomes much more akin to space, for space is a dimension that can be measured. Space can be measured, Deleuze claims, in ways that time cannot. Thus, to "measure" time is to treat time as though it were space. Therefore, Deleuze argues, if I measure time in that sort of way, that is, in terms of the "time covered" or the "time traveled," then I am actually conceiving of time in spatial terms. I am not conceiving of time *as* time. Rather, I am conceiving of time as though it were space. To clarify things to a further degree: if I conceive of time in terms of a sort of "distance covered" then I am actually conceiving of time as a form of movement. That is, the kind of question I am asking of time is akin to the sort of question I would ask when measuring movement. Movement is measured by asking How far is it from one point in space to another? To conceive of time in terms of movement is thus to ask this sort of question of time: How long does it take to get from the past to the present? Or: How long does it take to get from A to B? Or: How has time moved in such a way as to make the path from the past to the present clear and complete? Conceiving of time in this way is actually to conceive of time as a form of movement. And, for the cinema, to conceive of time in terms of movement is to give us a film characterized by what Deleuze calls the movement-image. The kind of timeline displayed in a film like *La signora di tutti* is therefore one that shows us a movement-image rather than a time-image. What occurs in such a film is that time is portrayed as a movement between past and present, where points between past, present, and future are fixed and clearly placed on a timeline. As a result, we know how the film's present came to be, such that it was caused by certain events that happened in the past: Gaby has committed suicide because she realizes her mistake in the past of choosing Leonardo instead of Roberto.

If films of the movement-image show time as a kind of movement, what Deleuze calls "an indirect image of time," then what does the time-image do to time? How does the time-image gives us a "direct image of time" or, as Deleuze claims, "A little time in the pure state"? (see C2, pp. 270–3).

The Past Can Change

Let us once again try to find our bearings, for if the movement-image has so far begun to feel rather complicated, then the time-image will, in fact, turn out to be somewhat more complicated again. Therefore, let us try some clear formulations. If the movement-image endeavors to fix the past-present-future into a clear, chronological order, then the time-image provides a far looser sense of chronological time and much more of a sense of lived time or time-as-it-is-experienced. This means that the time-image introduces relationships between the present and the past that are not fixed. Or, to try to put matters as simply as possible, for the time-image, the past can and does change its relationship to the present. *The past can change*: this is the major breakthrough initiated by the time-image. The past is not fixed.

But how can the past change? Isn't the past precisely that which cannot be changed? Isn't that one of the things that makes it the past, the blunt fact that it happened and now there's nothing that can be done to change that? We certainly see this, in *La signora di tutti*, via Gaby's decision to choose Leonardo over Roberto: she made the decision and has to suffer the consequences; there's nothing that can be done to change that decision and its consequences. The past is fixed, and surely that's what the past is. So how can the past change?

We need to consider that this is not the only way of conceiving of the past. Certainly, the *facts* of the past cannot be changed—say, that the Bastille was stormed on July 14, 1789. What can change, however, are the ways that an event from the past influences the present. The storming of the Bastille, and the French Revolution that followed it, has variously been interpreted as an eruption of dangerous passions that led inevitably to the Terror or 1792–4, as in Edmund Burke's *Reflections on the Revolution in France*, or as one of the glorious founding events of modern democracy, as expressed, in some ways, by Tocqueville's *The Ancient Regime and the French Revolution*. And historians will no doubt continue to research the French Revolution and discover new ways of thinking about it and conceiving of its history and effects. François Furet's intervention in the 1970s was startling in this respect: seeing the revolution as a founding moment for historians of the left and right, he also emphasized its role for left historians in the twentieth century as founding a myth of the future revolution.³ At any rate, approaches to and interpretations of the French Revolution will continue to go back into the past so as to reconceive of that past. In many ways, this is precisely what cinema is for Deleuze: it is a machine for going back into the past. For the movement-image, going back into the past is a way of fixing what happened in the past, of being certain about it, and thus of making clear connections between the past and the present. For the time-image, by contrast, one goes back into the past, but one is uncertain what one will find there, and the past will prove to be changeable and—perhaps even more provocatively—open to invention.

I have argued that *La signora di tutti* provides an example of a movement-image rather than a time-image. And yet, some aspects of the time-image may well be present there; that is, some aspects of the past as malleable or open to invention might be said to occur in *La signora di tutti*. For example, most of the film is framed as a flashback from Gaby's perspective. She has attempted suicide and has been rushed to a hospital. As the hospital staff place her under a gas-induced general anesthetic, by virtue of a large mask that is placed over the whole of her face, Gaby, on the verge of death, begins to remember significant episodes from her past. We thus are led to presume that everything we see from then on as viewers is solely from Gaby's perspective. It is possible, therefore, that her sense of being "everybody's lady"—that is, beautiful to the degree that men find her irresistible—is a perspective that is entirely her own. The same event seen from another character's perspective might offer up a substantially different account of the past. Add to this the fact that these memories are coming to us from a woman who is unconscious and on the verge of death, then we may have to accept that parts of her account are distorted or embellished. The past, as Gaby conceives it here, may be substantially or even entirely fictional, perhaps a dream-induced fiction (in the manner of The Wizard of Oz (Victor Fleming, 1939) or Woman in the Window (Fritz Lang, 1944)).

Consider also that, late in the film, after she has become a famous film star, as part of an event in which aspects of

Gaby's life are being celebrated, an event titled "Everybody's lady: Gaby Doriot talks about her life," her manager suggests to Gaby that she cannot talk about her real life, for it is too depressing and rife with scandal and intrigue. Rather, he urges her to make up a range of stories, stories that will be attractive to her fans. So who is to say that the memories we have been watching have not also been "made up" as simply one version of any number of possible pasts? Here, then, we have a very specific gesture toward the past as something that can be altered so as to suit the needs of the present (the manager's desire for publicizing of Gaby's life and career). To this degree *La signora di tutti* might be said to veer in the direction of the time-image.

Furthermore, *La signora* contains a startlingly inventive use of flashbacks (remembering this is a film made in 1934). Occasionally, as the film segues from one episode of Gaby's past to another, we will end one sequence with a character reflecting on what has been happening, only for this character's same account to continue as the action jumps forward in time where a new segment of the past in introduced. Or there are sections of the film that are not from Gaby's perspective. This occurs primarily during a sequence in which Leonardo appears before the board of directors of the company he owns and runs. He has shown up at this meeting after having spent several months traveling in Europe with Gaby, a chief expression of their whirlwind romance. It turns out that Leonardo has been using company money to fund this extended romantic holiday, so that the board is keen to make criminal charges against him. They eventually do so, and Leonardo is imprisoned for four years. And yet, Gaby was not present at this board meeting, even though we are supposed to presume we are still watching something akin to her flashback. We are therefore seeing Leonardo's version of events, events at which Gaby was not present and which she fairly likely did not know the details of. Even though these flashbacks are supposed to be Gaby's memories, we here have the interjection of several other people's versions of events which intersect with those of Gaby. In short, it becomes difficult to tell where one person's memories end and another's begin.

This kind of blending or "mixing up" of memories is a characteristic of the time-image: false memories, or memories that cannot be verified, memories of events that may or may not have happened. Where the movement-image tends to impart certainty to specific events in the past as well as to the effects of those events, uncertainty about the past is characteristic of the time-image. The movement-image creates direct cause-and-effect links between the past and the present, whereas for the time-image cause-and-effect linkages between the past and the present tend to break down.

Nevertheless, one should not make too much of these issues in relation to *La signora di tutti*, for it is clear that this film remains primarily a film of the movement-image even if it does occasionally dally with aspects of the time-image. The chief aim of *La signora* is to identify a specific series of events that lead to Gaby's suicide attempt and ultimately to her death. Doing this is a matter of definitively sorting out the chronology of events, from the initial scandal caused when, as a schoolgirl, one of her teachers had fallen in love with her, up to the end point where Gaby discovers that Roberto has in fact married her sister and that they are very happily married (this is the immediate motivation for Gaby's suicide). Therefore, the movement-image achieves this: a clear timeline upon which the events of the past are fixed in ways that lead directly to the events of the present and the future. This is what typically happens in films of the movement-image.

There is no such thing as a *pure* movement-image. As Deleuze argues, the time-image was always implicit in the movement-image. And so too will certain elements of the movement-image be evident in films of the time-image. More broadly speaking, this is also a way of saying that the "indirect image of time"— time conceived in terms of measurement and movement—is an absolutely necessary and extremely useful way of conceiving of time, but that alongside this indirect conception of time there are a great many rewards in conceiving of "a little time in the pure state." Time-as-movement and time-as-time can comfortably coexist.

The Time-Image

What then is a time-image? As I have already stated, time-images have a "looser" sense of time, a conception of time as lived or experienced rather than measured or specified on a clock or calendar. But I have also stated that cause-and-effect relations between the past and the present (and the future) are much weaker in films of the time-image than they are for the movement-image. For the time-image, the past does not necessarily cause the present (or the future), at least not in any direct or straightforward way. I have also claimed that what is important for films of the time-image is a notion that the past can change (or be changed).

Deleuze can act very much as a guide here, for when writing of Ophuls's films he declares that, typically, the scenes of those films provide situations "where the characters belong to the real and yet play a role. In short," he continues, "it is the whole of the real, life in its entirety, which has become spectacle" (C2, 83–4). The point Deleuze is trying to make here is that films of the time-image tend to collapse the distinction between what is real and what is fake or imagined. If we expand this to consider the relationship between the past and the present, it means that the task of films of the time-image is not one of discovering whether what happened in the past was real or whether it was merely imagined or dreamed. The aim of the time-image is not to determine whether the past we are shown is true or false. Rather, it is to open up the past to a range of potential interpretations.

I gather these formulations will sound somewhat vague, so an example will be apt. In *La signora di tutti*—a movement-image film—one of the issues at stake for Gaby's memories of the past is the question of whether Leonardo or Roberto was her true love. Who did she *really* love? And we know, as Gaby herself comes to realize, that it was Roberto she really loved. This means that her love for Leonardo was a "fake" love, a love in which she was merely "playing a role," for Leonardo was rich and Gaby enjoyed the trappings of his wealth. One of the aims of *La signora* is thus to go into the past in order to clearly discover what was real, on the one hand, and what was fake or imagined, on the other. In that way, the events of the past can be clearly laid out on a timeline: Gaby's love for Roberto represents a real or true past, while her love for Leonardo now exists as a fake past. Once this is established, the events of the past can have their effects clearly related to the present and the future: Gaby commits suicide because she realizes she has lost her true love. It is in this fashion that films of the movement-image expose clear and determinate links between past, present, and future.

Things are substantially different for films of the time-image. Let us take another of Ophuls's films, *La Ronde*, made in France in 1950. This—in some ways like *La signora di tutti*—is a film about love and about the past. But the task of *La Ronde* is not one of distinguishing true from false love. Rather, it is a celebration of the many different types and circumstances of love, and the question as to whether any of these loves is true or false, real or fake, is simply not an issue. That is not the kind of question this film asks. In a film like *La Ronde*, it is "the whole of the real," as Deleuze puts it, "which has become spectacle" (C2, 84). What can Deleuze possibly mean by claiming that, in a film like *La Ronde*, the "whole of the real has become spectacle"? Well, if what is at stake for films of the movement-image is to distinguish the true past from the false past, to separate the real from the fake, then no such aim is accorded the time-image. Instead, the time-image aims to show us the many possibilities the past may hold. One way to think of this is to consider that films of the time-image want to subject the past to a range of potential interpretations, not in order to then discover a "true" interpretation, but rather to see what effects and resonances emerge from the many potentialities of the past.

To fail to discover a "true" interpretation of the past—I tend to imagine that readers at this point must be saying to themselves why anybody would want to do that. Surely a logic whereby one discovers what really happened in the past is more important than vague assertions about the potentiality of the past—what Deleuze will eventually call the *virtuality* of the past. And yet, there are strong reasons for Deleuze's enthusiasm for a principle of multiple views of the past, where the task of going into the past is not one of distinguishing a true from a false past, but is instead a journey into the past "as spectacle." And the reason is this: if the past is fixed in such a way that a true or real past is revealed, then this implies that a true cause of the present has also been discovered: "and *that* is how the present came to be as it is." Furthermore, it implies that certain effects in the future will be fixed: "if *this* happened in the past, then *that* will happen in the future." Thus, for Deleuze to suggest the possibility of opening up the past, of not fixing the past, and thus of making the past susceptible to change, is also a way of ensuring that the present and the future will also be open to change. If the past is multiple and variable then so too will the present and future be multiple and variable. Such a conception is a central principle of the time-image.

Deleuze makes some interesting claims as to how all of this can happen. For example, he claims that we go back into the past in order to find our memories and dreams there. This means that, for Deleuze (and he relies very much on the writings of Henri Bergson in making these points), our memories do not take us back to the past, rather, we go into the past in order to then build our memories and dreams there. This is a way of reconstituting what the past was (or might have been, or could be). Deleuze writes, "It is in the past as it is in itself, as it is preserved in itself, that we go to look for our dreams and recollections, not the opposite" (*C2*, 80). How can such a thing happen? Let's take an example. Let's say I have lost my hat. I will ask myself "Where did I put it? Where did I last have it?" I thus place myself back into the past to imagine or remember where I last had my hat. Was it yesterday when I was in my car? Or was it when I was walking along the street the day before that? This is an example of going back into the past in order to discover what kinds of potentialities—or virtualities—the past can give rise to (Was it yesterday? Or the day before that? Or . . .?).

La Ronde

In many ways this is what happens in *La Ronde*. In the film we go back into the past to see what we might find there. Our guide through the events of this film, a character I will refer to as the MC, the "Master of Ceremonies," played by Anton Walbrook, begins the film by directly addressing the camera and asking "Where are we?" He speculates that we might be in a film set—we see props and lighting rigs, for example. He also tells us that he doesn't see reality only from one side, but that he sees it from all sides, "in the round (*à la ronde*)." So, first of all, the MC is inviting us to consider that what we are seeing, and are about to see, is not a reality fixed from one perspective, but a reality or series of realities that will be contemplated from a number of angles and points of view. This is our first hint that this film's journey will not be one of discovering a true real, but of contemplating the "real as spectacle."

The MC's next gesture is to place the action of the film in the past. We are in Vienna and the year is 1900, he tells us. "I adore the past," he says. "It's so much more peaceful than the present . . . and so much more certain than the future." Even as he gestures toward the certainties of the past, what then follows is a playful series of tales of love and lust which demonstrate the openness and inventiveness of the past. *La Ronde* is composed of a series of ten episodes in which each episode presents a love affair. As the actions of these love affairs progress, it transpires that for each of the couples, one member of the couple will subsequently, in the following episode, go on to have an affair with someone else. The film is therefore a series of love affairs and partner swaps. It is a celebration of love, lust, and infidelity and is thus rather a long way away from the search for true love that defines a film like *La signora di tutti*.

The episodes of *La Ronde* occur in the following order:

1 The girl (Léocadie) and the soldier
2 The soldier and the maid
3 The maid and the young man
4 The young man and the married woman
5 The married woman and her husband
6 The married man and the little woman
7 The little woman and the poet
8 The poet and the actress
9 The actress and the Count
10 The Count and the girl (Léocadie)

Here we can see how the love affairs jump from one episode to the next such that the soldier of the first episode then has an affair with the maid in the second episode, and then in the third episode this same maid will have an affair with a young man, and so on until we return to the beginning, as it were, when the Count has an affair with the young girl, Léocadie, from whom all the affairs began.

The logic of the film is one of fecundity and expansion, of interlinking and crossing over. Above all, we can call this a principle of multiplicity. In this respect, the form of *La Ronde* differs markedly from *La signora di tutti*, for the latter offers a principle of choosing between alternatives rather than a principle of multiplicity. How does a principle of multiplicity work? It works by establishing connections. Therefore, instead of rationalizing and clarifying connections so that one might discover a true connection—as happens in *La signora di tutti*—a principle of multiplicity is followed in *La Ronde* whereby connections are expanded and multiplied. Instead of a logic of choosing between a true and a false love, *La Ronde* shows us how one love affair turns into another affair, then another, and so on. This notion of connecting and expanding exemplifies a principle of multiplicity.

And yet, we are once again back to the question: Why is this a time-image? What does a principle of multiplicity have to do with time or a time-image? Let us consider how this works. Films of the movement-image, like *La signora di tutti*, unfold on a timeline that leads to a definite conclusion. Such conclusions tend to leave us with a consideration of the ways that the "true" has now been distinguished from the "false." In *La signora*, Gaby discovers, finally, that Roberto had been the true destiny of her love. In this way, films of the movement-image tend to follow classic narrative patterns of closure. Such a narrative pattern also provides a specific model of time. And we have already seen this: *La signora* shows us a model of time in which the past, present, and future are clearly positioned and fixed such that the events of the past (Gaby's wrong choice in love) can be said to have caused the present situation (Gaby's suicide attempt) and future (her death).

The narrative trajectory of *La Ronde* and other films of the time-image is typically different from this. The trajectory of *La Ronde* is not based on a clear timeline where "facts" can be arranged in their appropriate order. Rather, one event folds into another: one event does not cause or lead to another, but events happen and connections emerge in ways that are not destined or predictable. Rather, events occur and it is their occurring that is important, not why they happened (a "cause"), or what they will then lead to (as an "effect"), but just the sheer *that* of their happening.

A Little Stroll Through Time

The openness of *La Ronde*'s narrative is accompanied by a specific sense that what we are seeing is more or less fabricated—as Deleuze puts it, where "the whole of the real has become spectacle." *La Ronde* therefore offers a very different approach to the real, or the true, than does *La signora di tutti*. Where the latter film is built on an earnest search for the truth, that is, a search for what "really happened" in the past, *La Ronde*, by contrast, is playful and gives the impression of being fake or fabricated. How does *La Ronde* do this? First of all, the MC begins the film somewhat arbitrarily, declaring that we are in Vienna in the year 1900, but also suggesting that we could be anywhere, as though he has chosen simply to set the action here on a whim, for no particular reason. And it will transpire that for the remainder of the film the MC will act as a kind of manipulator of events. Primarily this is achieved by way of "la ronde" itself: the merry-go-round the MC introduces us to very early in the film's introductory sequence. The merry-go-round is itself a figure of play—it is "fun" and "frivolous"—but it also acts as a spinning wheel (a roulette wheel or "wheel of fortune"): round and round it spins, where it will stop, no one can be sure.

And so the merry-go-round/la ronde is, throughout the film, a figure of frivolity and arbitrariness. It is not a figure of the true or real. At the same time, the merry-go-round offers an allegory of the cinematic mechanism, for its spinning is akin to that of a film reel spinning through a projector. It also becomes clear at many points during the film that the MC is a stand-in for a film director or auteur. It is *he* who makes the film, as it were, and often he will guide characters or manipulate events in order to facilitate their consequences. There are many examples of this. In the second episode, "The soldier and the maid," the MC intervenes in order to lead the maid—her name is Marie (played by Simone Simon)—away from the dance she is attending with the soldier (Serge Reggiani). In taking her away from the soldier, he thereby leads her toward *La Ronde*'s third episode, "The maid and the young man." As he leads her away from the dance he tells her there is a good chance she will have been dismissed by her employer for having stayed out so late at night. As a consequence, the MC therefore leads the maid to her next job. In doing so, he tells her, "Two months from now, fate will be very kind to you." To this Marie than asks, "Where are you taking me?" and he gives her the remarkable response, "We are taking a little stroll through time." (What better indicator of the time-image could one ask for?) And verily they stroll forward two months in time to where Marie is now the maid in a new household.

As if that were not enough, after he has introduced Marie to her new household, the MC then begins to sing a melody that recurs throughout the film—a kind of "theme of la ronde"—and he walks away from the maid's household, a household that is also quite clearly a film set. He then enters a large room where a small orchestra is playing the accompaniment to his song. We are therefore clearly in the realm of spectacle, fabrication, artifice: any search for the truth or the real is here rendered null. To round matters off, the MC then holds up a cinematic clapper board upon which the title of *La Ronde*'s third episode is written: "The maid and the young man."

Another point at which the MC manipulates *La Ronde*'s events in ways that associate him with the film's authorship occurs in the film's penultimate episode, "The actress and the Count." As these two figures—played by Isa Miranda (star of *La signora*) and Gérard Philipe—fall into an embrace on the actress's bed with the intention of making love, the camera elaborately tilts upward so as to capture their embrace reflected in a mirror above the bed. There is then an abrupt cut, and the next image is of the MC holding a strip of film reel which he is cutting up with scissors at various points. The MC is thus intervening so as to avoid the ire of the censors: the sexual acts are, of course, edited out! The MC's dismissive murmur here is, "Ahhh, censorship!"

In short, *La Ronde* exhibits a tone or attitude that is far removed from that of *La signora di tutti*. In standard film studies parlance such moments as I have described would most likely be called "reflexive." Matters of reflexivity are not, however, of concern for Deleuze. But if reflexivity is not an issue for Deleuze, what are we to make of these scenes? And—once again—why would Deleuze argue that these kinds of cinematic gestures are ones associated with the time-image?

The Regimes of Images

If Deleuze is not interested in notions of reflexivity, then what are his ways of justifying the distinction between the movement-image and the time-image? In other words, what is the point of the movement-image, and what is the point of the time-image? Films of the movement-image, as I have already claimed, tend to move their actions toward a definitive conclusion. They find solutions to the problems that arise in their plots. Such is the case even in a film with a decidedly negative ending, such as occurs in *La signora di tutti* with Gaby's suicide (and it is worth noting that this is a factor—the death or impending death of a lead female character—that will be repeated across a range of Ophuls's films). Gaby's suicide provides an answer and conclusion to various problems that emerge in the film's plot—that is, that Gaby had been foolish to have chosen Leonardo instead of Roberto and that her life now seems a consequence of this poor choice. What this demonstrates is that films of the movement-image tend to make the present a clear consequence of events that have happened in the past: the present is explained by the past. All of this is part of a tendency for films of the movement-image to arrange their "facts" clearly on a timeline upon which events are fixed. On that timeline, "false" events will be clearly distinguished from "true" ones, so that at the end of *La signora* we come to the realization that the love Gaby believed she held for Leonardo was a false love. And so too do we learn that the love she felt for Roberto must have been true. With those elements made clear—for that is what really happened in the past; that was the true meaning of the past—the actions of the film can be clearly fixed in time. The true events of the past—Gaby's now unrequited love for Roberto—can be said to have definitively caused the present events in which Gaby has attempted suicide. And perhaps that is the most succinct way to conceive of the significance of the movement-image: *the past causes the present*. (By association, the past will then also be the cause of the future.)

By contrast, for films of the time-image, *the past remains open*. It may seem that such a statement is not especially advantageous, for it is immensely useful for us to take lessons from the past and to understand that actions and choices made in the past can help us to act and choose in the present (and future). I have known from past actions that an attempt to touch a burning flame is painful, so I know now in the present to avoid such actions. These kinds of choices in which the fixed truths of the past determine what we can or should do in the present and future are utterly essential for our existence—indeed, it is probably fair to say that the vast majority of human actions and decisions proceed on such terms. In that case, what advantage can there be to keeping the past open? What advantage can there be in declaring that the past can change? And furthermore, then, what is the point of the time-image?

The best way to conceive of this problem is to admit that the past can be closed down, and to some degree, this is not a good thing at all. And yet, closing down the past is certainly not all bad. For mundane acts such as avoiding burning flames or knowing that one gets wet when it rains or acquiring the skill of riding a bicycle, definitively knowing what has happened in the past can be a great asset. The kind of knowledge gained from events and actions such as these might well be aspects of knowledge that can be "closed down": we know them, and acting on them brings great advantages to our lives. But things become more complicated if we take more complex examples, such as the storming of the Bastille in 1789. If this event from the past is interpreted as a gross insurrection by the rabble, then it will follow that any such action by the lower classes in the present or the future which involves insurrection might also be labeled as wrong and thus subject to punishment. By contrast, if the event is seen as being the first step freedom for oppressed peoples, then such acts of insurrection will be seen as ways in which, in the present or future, oppressed people can rise up against their masters and so overturn their state of oppression. These are both examples of ways in which the past can be closed down: to declare that this happened (the storming of the Bastille), and its significance is thus (either a gross insurrection or a step toward freedom), is to deny other possible interpretations and possible avenues for present and future acts. One task for humans, therefore, is to avoid closing down the past, to keep it open for new possibilities of interpretation and consideration. And we know that historians—and others—will continue to debate the virtues and otherwise of the French Revolution that resulted from the storming of the Bastille. This involves a continual placing oneself back into the past so as to reimagine and reconceive what occurred there, to find new possibilities in what one finds there by going back into the past. In short, it requires keeping the past open.

Another way to conceive of this distinction between closing down the past and keeping the past open is to consider that human beings and human societies can get very used to doing things in certain ways—call these habits or customs. Arguments proposed by French philosopher Michel Foucault, a thinker who exerted a profound influence on Deleuze (so much so that he wrote a book, *Foucault*, dedicated to his work), can bring us to the core of the issues here: how do ideas, practices, and beliefs become embedded over time, and then how does it happen that those practices can change?[4] Across a range of books Foucault charted the ways that historical practices and beliefs will often undergo radical revisions so that what was once accepted as being a normal or typical way of doing something all of a sudden becomes altered so that a new practice comes to replace it. In his *History of Madness* (published in 1961 in France as *Folie et deraison*), for example, Foucault traced the ways that, in French medical practice, as well as in philosophy and legal theory, the category of "madness" came to be defined in the late seventeenth and eighteenth centuries in ways that were distinctly different from what the term "madness" had previously designated.[5] The concept of madness changed its meaning and, in doing so, instituted a new range of ideas concerning what it was to be mad—that a mad person was excluded from reasonable discourse and society, and would be subject to medical and legal treatments, for example. Much of Foucault's account here is also one that traces how the notion of reason took hold during this period too, such that reason became one of the defining traits of what it was to be a true and proper human being, with the consequence that those designated mad could be considered somewhat less than human (and in need of some kind of treatment so as to try to make them more properly human). The upshot of all this is that what was now deemed mad had not always been called this, and so too what came to be called reason was very much a historically determined emergence: reason itself changed, as it were, from the seventeenth to the eighteenth century (often known to us as the Age of Reason).

Foucault is trying to highlight the ways in which our very conceptions of the world, of how the world works, and even of what "people" are, of what makes a human being a human being, can change. An even more famous example of this kind of change was mapped out by Foucault in terms of a transition in notions of criminal punishment and imprisonment from the late eighteenth into the nineteenth century. In his book called *Discipline and Punish* (first published in 1975), Foucault argued that the practices of criminal punishment changed during this period so that, where previously criminals had typically been punished by way of overt bodily injury—such as having one's fingers chopped off as a punishment for theft—at the end of the nineteenth century it became more accepted for criminals to be placed in prison rather than to be physically punished.[6] The logic of this practice of confinement, Foucault argued, was that prisoners would seek a kind of interior punishment: instead of an overt bodily display featuring torture and external punishment of the body—Foucault's chapter here is called "The Spectacle of the Scaffold"—punishment was now supposed to be internal; one's soul or mind or behavior was now supposed to undergo an internal reformation rather than endure an external marking. Again Foucault reckons this to be an indicator of changes in the ways that human beings themselves were conceived. In other words, what truly came to define what human beings were was a matter of their internal thoughts, their capacities for self-reflection which would enable their behaviors and beliefs to be in accord with social expectations. Allied to this, of course, was the belief that criminals could be reformed such that their behavior would be brought into line with society's expectations of normal behavior.

From One Regime to Another

It might seem as though we have wandered away from our consideration of the movement-image and the time-image. The point of the earlier discussion of the work of Foucault is, however, twofold. We have asked: how does historical change occur? How does one set of circumstances change and thus give rise to another set of circumstances, a new way of doing things? Insofar as they offer perspectives on the past, a first consideration is that, as I have already claimed, films of the movement-image tend to close down the past, while films of the time-image keep the past open. This distinction offers something of a simplification—Deleuze himself never made such a claim. Most films of both image regimes provide models of change, that is, of how one set of circumstances alters in some way such that a new set of circumstances comes into being. (Alternatively, a narrative might instead begin with a set of circumstances which is subsequently disrupted—typically called a narrative's development or complication—such that narrative closure is achieved when the original set of circumstances is returned to.) If a new set of circumstances comes into being, then films of the movement-image will present these rather differently than will films of the time-image. Films of the movement-image will present those circumstances in ways that are definitive: they will provide a definitive answer to whatever problem is set in train by the film's narrative.

In *La signora di tutti*, for example—an example of the movement-image—the narrative initially establishes a problem: why has Gaby Doriot tried to kill herself? This problem can be couched in terms of Gaby's transformations as the film progresses: from that of a schoolgirl whose future is curtailed by a romantic scandal involving one of her teachers—a teacher who commits suicide as a consequence of his forbidden love for Gaby—through to her relationships with her sister, with Roberto, and his mother, Alma, and thence to her affair with Leonardo. Finally, following the collapse of Leonardo's business affairs and his imprisonment, Gaby takes up an acting career where she finds fame and fortune, if not happiness. The film's final act of restaging the past occurs when Gaby discovers that Roberto has married her sister, Anna, and that Anna has found the happiness Gaby was unable to find. It is here, then, that the narrative provides a solution to its original problem: Why has Gaby attempted suicide? Because she failed to find love and happiness.

It is important to note the ways in which *La signora di tutti*, with its stunning use of flashbacks, eventually organizes its events on a timeline such that each event contributes to a conception of *how things are in the present*. In doing so, the film is an exercise in showing us *how things came to be the way they are*. The consequence of this is that, even though there are changes throughout the film—and how can there not be? Gaby's changes of heart; Leonardo's changes of circumstance; Roberto's transfer of feelings from Gaby to Anna; and so on— these changes are presented as though they are preplanned: all the events of the past have happened in such a way that they inevitably lead to the conditions of the present. (They will also lead, eventually, to the future and to Gaby's death at the very end of the film.)

La Ronde is different, which is a way of saying that the time-image opens up relationships to the past and to change that are markedly different from those of the movement-image. One way to think of *La Ronde* is to ask: what is the problem this film sets up and what answers to this problem does *La Ronde* discover? And immediately here we come across a conception of the past and change that is very different from *La signora di tutti* and other films of the movement-image. Films of the time-image do not typically organize themselves according to a problem-solution formation. Rather, the shape of *La Ronde* is altogether more open than is *La signora*. *La Ronde* takes us back into the past, but with no particular agenda or aim other than to go back into the past in order to explore. And what do we find there? We find a range of tales and rendezvous that would typically have remained hidden—these are "forbidden tales," as it were. We find flings and romances that are "not on the public record." In other words, we discover events that would have been written out of "standard" histories.

If we were to push a little harder we might say that the problem posed by *La Ronde* relates to love: What is love? If this is posed as a problem then certainly no definitive answer is provided. Rather, multiple answers are given: each of the ten episodes is, in one way or another, presenting us with a conception of love. The passionate lust of a young soldier gives us one version, the playful adventures of a young maid another, the deceptions and schemes of an older married couple yet another, and so on. If films of the movement-image endeavor to provide a definitive solution to a problem posed by the film's plot, then films of the time-image, by contrast, provide multiple solutions to the problems raised by their plots (if, indeed, such things as "problems" emerge at all).

A second point on historical change to take from Foucault: how do we move from one historical period to another? For example, how do we move from a point in history where madness means one thing, to a point in history where madness begins to mean something else? Foucault's answer very much amounts to resisting any specific reason for such changes. Rather than attributing any specific cause-and-effect logic to such historical changes—that the reason madness changed its meaning was because of x—Foucault is content to declare that this change did happen, but also that no one has noted that this change occurred, and that the change occurred without any sense of historical destiny or meaning. (Foucault also makes his case convincing by drawing on a vast amount of evidence to back up his claims.) All of this is a way of claiming that events or situations are not necessarily caused by events that happened in the past. In short, it is a way of arguing that historical change does not, or does not necessarily, follow a cause-and-effect logic. Sometimes change simply happens (and very often it happens without us even noticing it).

Such conceptions of historical change are important for Deleuze's consideration of the transition from the movement-image to the time-image. I have already claimed that, generally speaking, the movement-image was dominant from the period of early cinema up until the Second World War, while films of the time-image began to emerge during and after the Second World War (again noting that this is a rough guide). So why did films of the time-image begin to emerge at around this point in history? There might certainly be some reasons, chiefly creative ones; that is, that filmmakers were looking for expanding and extending the creative possibilities of film. But even to declare this much is not to point to a specific cause which would explain why films of the time-image began to come into being. Rather, Deleuze's aim is to convincingly prove that, at around the period of the Second World War, some filmmakers began to make a variety films the likes of which had not been made before, films that took time, memory, and the past as major tropes. In short, making a different kind of film—a "time-image"—became possible at around the period of the Second World War, though it is not entirely clear why this happened. That it did happen is something Deleuze endeavors to prove in his *Cinema* books.

Deleuze and Philosophy: Nietzsche

Thus far I have attempted to make this book relatively free from philosophical jargon and debates. The opening pages, especially the discussions of *La signora di tutti* and *La Ronde*, have laid out the central stakes of Deleuze's *Cinema* books, especially foregrounding the distinction between the movement-image and the time-image. All of this has been done using the plainest language possible. To some extent I will now need to alter my approach somewhat in order to incorporate some fairly complex philosophical discussions. Deleuze's writings are notoriously difficult, for he often assumes his readers will possess a fairly sophisticated knowledge of the history of philosophy (and of art, literature, and cinema). In what follows I detail some key aspects of Deleuze's approach to philosophy. Deleuze's philosophy often utilizes arguments made by past philosophers, and here I concentrate on three of those: Friedrich Nietzsche (1844–1900), Baruch Spinoza (1632–77), and Henri Bergson (1859–1941). Bergson is especially important for the *Cinema* books, for these books are in part a commentary on Bergson's philosophy: there are two "commentaries" on Bergson in each of the books. Another point I will foreground here concerns the matter of how Deleuze approaches the question of human subjectivity: What is a human being? What is a subject? And what kinds of subjects are important for films and cinema?

I begin with Nietzsche, arguably the most important philosophical influence on Deleuze. The significance of Nietzsche's thought for Deleuze, especially in relation to the *Cinema* books, can be summarized via three key concepts as follows:

1 Become who you are
2 A revaluation of all values
3 The eternal return

Become who you are. What might Nietzsche mean when, in *Thus Spoke Zarathustra*, he has Zarathustra exclaim, "Become who you are!"?[7] Or when in *The Gay Science* Nietzsche remarks that "you shall become the person you are"?[8] Or what is his aim in subtitling *Ecce Homo* "How One Becomes What One Is"?[9] Nietzsche makes this matter of "becoming who one is" central to his philosophy quite simply because he believes very few people reach their full potential. Becoming who you are entails, to a large extent, rejecting what you have been and therefore reinventing yourself to become something other than what you have been. As he puts it right at the beginning of *On the Genealogy of Morality*, "We are unknown to ourselves . . . . We have never looked for ourselves" (p. 3).[10] Nietzsche's point is that we are used to doing things and believing in things that we have never fully endorsed on our own terms. We tend to do things because "that's the way things are," or because "that's the way we have done it in the past." We do things out of habit or custom, or merely because someone else has told us to do those things. Nietzsche therefore contends that we rarely do something because we genuinely believe in it. We rarely do anything as a result of having a genuine conviction in doing it, a genuine belief or sense that doing *this* matters, and in such a way that it matters to *me*, above all else; that I am not doing something because it matters to my boss, my teacher, my parents, or whoever, but rather that I am doing it because it matters to *me*.

In his 1962 book on Nietzsche, Deleuze presents these issues in terms of a distinction between active and reactive forces.[11] Active forces are those that we have full faith in, that we endorse unashamedly and which, therefore, strengthen us and enable us to overcome our weaknesses and vulnerabilities. The aim of a Nietzschean philosophy is, claims Deleuze, to maximize our active forces. Against those active forces, reactive forces are those we do not endorse ourselves, but are instead reactions to what others do to us. As such, they are forces that do not originate in us, but are lesser or secondary forces that weaken us and prevent us from becoming better people: they prevent you from becoming who you are.

The advocacy of active forces links with the second point from Nietzsche: a revaluation of all values. The values that have been passed down to us, Nietzsche argues, are ones that have foregrounded reactive forces; they are moral values that have severely restricted the progress of humankind and have therefore fostered weakness and mediocrity rather than strength and brilliance. And they are like this simply because they have been passed down to us: we have not determined our morality for ourselves. Rather, we are typically content with accepting the moral worldviews that have been passed down to us. And so, in *On the Genealogy of Morality*, published in 1887, he will declare, "We need a critique of moral values."[12] Nietzsche argues that we are far too used to following the crowd, accepting a world that is defined by others, by "experts," rule-makers, and lawgivers, rather than creating and defining a world on our own terms.

Nietzsche might sound bombastic here, but the brilliance of Deleuze's reading of him is to have foregrounded the distinction between active and reactive forces. Deleuze demonstrates the importance of reactive forces. There is no doubt that such forces are related to some of the key negative themes in Nietzsche's philosophy, *ressentiment* and *nihilism*, for it is an excess of reactive forces that results in these negative factors. *Ressentiment* is a negative outlook on the world that forever condemns the world, and which fails to find any positive solution or way out of this condemnation—just think of the kind of person who is always complaining about the state of the world or their life, but never doing anything about it. "*Ressentiment* is the triumph of the weak *as* weak," Deleuze writes.[13] Nihilism is the great theme of Nietzsche's later years, a conviction that the overt moralism and rule-making of the age have resulted in a thoroughgoing negativity, a world of resignation. There is, however, a positive side to reactive forces, and it provides Deleuze's most important contribution to commentaries on Nietzsche. The formidable task for humankind, Deleuze argues, is to accept reactive forces in such a way as to turn them around so that they become active. Deleuze declares that "reactive forces only triumph by going to the limit of their consequences, that is, by becoming an active force."[14] Nietzsche's position, therefore, is one of rising up against the reactive forces that restrict human ambition and greatness, and turning those reactive forces into active ones.

And yet, what does this ability to turn reactive forces into active ones have to do with the final principle to be taken from Nietzsche, that of the famous "eternal return"? The notion of the eternal return is immediately linked with the preceding points, for it declares that one ought to be worthy of one's actions, that one's actions should matter to the extent that one would be willing for those actions to be repeated eternally. This introduces, for Nietzsche, a rather complicated relationship with time. To revert to the kind of language we have already been using, it requires an "open" approach to time and to history, not a relationship to time that is "closed down." The great interpreter of this aspect of Nietzsche's thought is, once again, Foucault, who argued that Nietzsche's approach to history positioned itself against those versions of history that sought to, in Foucault's words, "compose the finally reduced diversity of time to a totality fully closed upon itself."[15] This kind of history—Nietzsche called it "monumental" history—would be a "complete" history where every event has its place and every event is in its place in such a way that the past inevitably leads to the present and to the future. From such a perspective it is as though the past were secretly controlling and predetermining the present and the future. Such versions of the past, and thus of time, demonstrate a resistance to change—as Foucault puts it, a "totality fully closed upon itself"—and for Nietzsche these are prime indicators of the reactive forces of a weak morality.

What does one therefore do with history and the past? Nietzsche advocates what he calls forgetting—not forgetting as such, but of turning parts of the past against themselves so that they no longer determine the future. In other words, what Nietzsche is arguing is that, to some degree, the past one has learned needs to be unlearned and, as a consequence, made new. Nietzsche calls this "critical" history: "man must possess and from time to time employ the strength to break up and dissolve a part of the past."[16] Such a strategy might be said to be against memory, but it is only against memory to the extent that one can be hindered or weighed down by the memories of one's past. Freeing oneself from those memories involves turning those memories around and against themselves—"forgetting" those memories, as it were—so that those memories can be replaced by a positive, new, "active" memory that will open up new, positive futures.

One other way in which Deleuze interprets Nietzsche's appeal to forgetting is to claim that active forces are associated with the body and reactive forces are associated with the mind (and so the mind is also associated with forms of consciousness and self-consciousness, as well as memory, and ultimately *ressentiment*). Thus, one way of overcoming reactive forces is to prioritize the activities of the body. In a straightforward sense, this is a call to do things rather than brooding over one's memories or regrets: doing rather than thinking. Perhaps a clearer way to suggest how such a process occurs is to consider that one can spend a long time considering what one might do or could do—reflecting, considering, "milling something over"—but one can only overcome such a state of reflection by actually doing something: continually brooding over some issue, declaring that things must change or that things "cannot go on like this" will most likely lead only to *ressentiment* and nihilism and thus to failure. Turning this resentment around so that an act is performed—this provides a way beyond reactive forces and thus toward the positivity of action.[17]

Deleuze and Philosophy: The Importance of Bergson

We have already introduced some elements of Bergson's philosophy, for much of Bergson's thought is central to Deleuze's *Cinema* books—indeed, these books are inconceivable without

Bergson. As was the case with Nietzsche, I will proceed via
three key concepts of Bergson's philosophy:

1 time as change
2 affection
3 the "subject" and memory

Time as change. "Time is invention, or it is nothing at
all,"[18] wrote Bergson, and we have already seen that his
most fundamental philosophical claim is that time cannot
be measured. Time is therefore not like space, for the latter
contains things which are measureable, according to Bergson
(see *CE*, 174–5). This means that the "clock time" we are
used to—minutes, seconds, hours, days, and so on—has little
to do with Bergson's conception of time. The clock time we
are used to—and let's face it, our lives, certainly in terms of
the ways that contemporary societies are organized, would
be unthinkable and unworkable without clock time: but
our lives would not be impossible without it; far from it, in
fact—is the result of a long history of abstraction, Bergson
argues. What is characteristic of this human tendency toward
abstraction is that of dividing the world into manipulable bits
of information. Such abstraction is a matter of reducing our
experiences to measurable chunks. Bergson is adamant that
such abstraction and measurement—a quantifying of life and
experience—has little to do with the actual ways in which
we experience the world. Bergson will go so far as to declare
that *"The intellect is characterized by a natural inability to
comprehend life"* (*CE*, 182). Against intellectual abstraction,
Bergson proposes a method of intuition. Intuition offers a way
of trying to account for the flow of life and experience—for
the flow of time, no less. And the flow of time is such that it is
difficult if not impossible to quantify. Time, far from being a
quantity, is instead a quality. Bergson will go on to claim that
life, consciousness, and "the way we experience the world" are
also qualities rather than measurable quantities. That might

be the defining trait of Bergson's philosophy: the quest to comprehend the quality of time.

We know that Deleuze came up with the notion of the time-image to account for some of the ways that certain kinds of films envisage time. A good way to understand what is essential to films of the time-image is to declare that they give us qualitative images of time: they show us time as a quality rather than as a quantity. It will sound sensible to declare then that, as distinct from films of the time-image, those of the movement-image can only show us time as a quantity, as measurement. And to some degree this is true (I have thus far argued as much in this book). But to push too far in this direction will be to overlook that movement too is a matter of flow and quality: movement moves, and in doing so it defies measurement and conditions of being quantified. What this means for Deleuze's account of cinema is that the movement-image—images-in-movement—brings with it an enormous philosophical potential: the possibility of countering abstract thought so as to replace it with a method of intuition. Movement, like time, is a matter of change.

One point worth making, however, is that things—objects, bodies—do stop moving, and so to consider the stopped motion of such objects is a very attractive thing to do. It enables us to get our bearings. We can measure the distances between objects when they stop moving. Bergson writes, "If the intellect were meant for pure theorizing, it would take its place within movement. . . . But the intellect is meant for something altogether different . . . , it takes the opposite course; it always starts from immobility" (CE, 171). All of this is of tremendous use for humankind, so much so that one commentator on Bergson states that "The intellect, which has evolved as an organ of utility, has a need for stability and reliability. It thus seeks connections and establishes stable and regular relations between transitory forces."[19] Stopping, measuring, taking stock, and charting a course are all very useful things for humans to do. But they are abstractions. Reducing all the world and the experiences of life to the conditions of stopped motion—immobility—is very much to abstract from the true conditions of the world. "*In short*," Bergson claims, "*the world the mathematician deals with is a world that dies and is reborn at every instant*" (CE, 26–7). We shall see that Bergson describes this mathematical conception of the world via the "cinematographic mechanism." Deleuze, however, creatively reinterprets Bergson's criticisms of the cinema apparatus so as to demonstrate that, in actuality, the cinematograph provides an excellent example of movement as such.

Duration and time—for Bergson these are all matters of change. But time does not merely or only imply succession. In other words, the unfolding of time is not merely a matter of how time apparently seems to go from the past through the present and into the future. The situation is, so Bergson claims, more complicated than this. The most important aspect of time for Bergson is that it is composed of a combination of the past and the present. Time *is* this combination of past and present. And yet, to complicate matters slightly more, time is both the combination of past and present and their splitting. Time is produced by the division between past and present. When the past "splits off" from the present, *that* is time. Memory therefore becomes crucial for Bergson's conceptions here, for the relationship between memory—*the past*—and perception—*the present*—is central for Bergson's account of time. It is also essential for understanding Deleuze's account of cinema. I clarify the stakes of the memory-past, perception-present combination as this book develops.

Before tackling that point, however, I want to consider the second key point to be taken from Bergson: affection. What are affects, and how are we affected by objects and events? Bergson begins by considering our bodies—human bodies—as things that we know not just externally, but that we also know *from the inside*. In fact, my body is unique in this respect, for other bodies and objects are things I can only know from the "outside"—I can see them and touch them, but I cannot know or feel them from the inside, as it were. My own body is something I can feel from the inside precisely because I am, in some sense, "inside" my body. Bergson navigates this terrain by distinguishing between my power to perceive and my power for affection—"my perception is outside my body and my affection within it," he writes (*MM*, 57).

But what, then, is affection? Bergson argues that affection is what occurs when an external body or thing intersects with my own body. Thus, being touched by something gives rise to affection. And yet, affection amounts to much more than this. It describes a conjunction between myself and another thing—a conjoining, which means that, however temporarily, external thing becomes part of what is inside me. It becomes something I feel from the inside. Via one of his most illuminating examples, that of being pricked by a pin, Bergson asks, "what, indeed, would be pain detached from the subject that feels it?" (*MM*, 53). Perception and affection go hand-in-hand, as we have already seen Bergson claim. This means that perception and affection are not easily separable. If Bergson claims that perception is outside and affection is inside my body, then he will also claim that "there is no perception without affection" (*MM*, 58). Why? He argues that when we see objects—a pin, for example—we also perceive such objects in terms of their potential action upon us. I perceive the potential for the pin to prick me, and thus in my perception of the pin is contained some measure of affection. "Affection is, then," writes Bergson, "that part or aspect of the inside of our body which we mix with *the image of* external bodies" (*MM*, 58, my emphasis).

All of this brings us to our central point here. Bergson's conception of the human subject is one that conceives of such subjects as irrevocably connected with—indeed, conjoined with—the objects and bodies that surround them and with which they come into contact. The "subject," for Bergson, is composed of my body and the things which my body comes into contact with. Therefore, if I am pricked by a pin, then that pin and the pain it produces in me become part of me. It is in this way that subjects are formed. Subjects are formed by virtue of the things they come into contact with. These contacts *are* the subject. At one point Bergson describes the brain as "a kind of central telephone exchange" insofar as "[i]t adds nothing to what it receives" (*MM*, 30). And we can conceive of the subject in precisely this way too: it adds nothing to what it receives, but rather *is* what it receives. The subject is merely a "meeting point" for various messages, bits of information, and affections that cross its path, that intersect with it, and which, in doing so, *are* the subject.

Bergson describes in some detail how this "exchange" functions. Perception, he argues, is dependent upon possible action. From everything that can be perceived, perception singles out those things that are most useful for it. My perceptual faculties do not perceive everything. Rather, my perception has the ability to focus on what is important for me to apprehend. If I am seeking to cross a road, for example, my perception will focus on the sight and sound of cars as they approach or recede from where I want to cross. I will therefore not even notice the small bird nestled in a tree on the other side of the road, and nor will I notice the barking of a dog in the distance. Rather, my perception will focus on the task at hand: crossing the road. So we single out aspects of perception that are useful to us, and we also isolate those aspects of perception that are related to action, that is, in this example, crossing the road.

What, then, does perception have to do with affection? Affection is concerned with *re*action. When I am pricked by a pin I react with a feeling of pain. After this, I will likely respond with an action such as placing my hand on the part of my body where the pin has pricked my skin. There will, of course, be a delay between the reaction and its consequent action. I will feel the pin prick and then subsequently act upon the pin or the place on my skin where the cut has occurred. This delay between the feeling of the pin prick and an action in consequence of this is a delay that is characteristic of affection. Affection is therefore a "feeling inside me" (affection per se) that will subsequently be related to an object "outside me," and my action upon it. And all of this emerges from the originating point of perception itself, with perception being the "fact," as it were, of the pin pricking the skin. Perception is the "it is happening" of the event (*a pin is entering my skin*), while the affection is the feeling of this event (*the feeling of pain as the pin pricks me*), and the action is my response to the event (*e.g., placing my hand where the pin has pricked me in an attempt to ease the pain*). Bergson states at one point that "perception measures the reflecting power of the body, [while] affection measures its power to absorb" (*MM*, 56). We will see later in this book, in relation to the time-image, just how important this delay of affection, this "power to absorb," becomes.

Bergson does not make a distinction between active and reactive in the way we have seen Nietzsche do. For Nietzsche active forces are generally ones that strengthen, while reactive forces are typically ones that give rise to weakness. Bergson claims, for his part, that every action is a reaction of some sort. Every action is a reaction to something that has been perceived. Thus, when aiming to cross the road, if I see that no cars are coming along that road, then my action will be to cross the road. This is an action—crossing the road—but it is also a reaction to my perceiving that the road is clear. But how does this actually happen? Who or what makes the decision to cross the road? Is it a "subject," and, if so, how does the subject "make" a decision? It is here that Bergson introduces the crucial point that brings together perception, affection, and memory. He writes that "the choice of reaction cannot be the work of chance. The choice is likely to be inspired by past experience, and the reaction does not take place without an appeal to the memories which analogous situations may have left behind them" (*MM*, 65). Actions and reactions, as well as perception, are thus linked with memory, and this is a very significant link to make.

Why is the link between perception and memory significant? It is significant because it makes perception a matter of time. Perception may seem to take place in the present, but Bergson argues that this is only part of the story. Rather, perception cannot help but be a combination of past and present. "These two acts," writes Bergson, "perception and recollection, always interpenetrate each other" (*MM*, 67). So we can now say that perception and affection are always linked ("there is no perception without affection") but so too are perception and memory inextricably linked (they "always interpenetrate each other").

Generally speaking, we can begin to consider these relationships in the following way:

external to the body	↔	inside the body
perception	↔	affection
perception	↔	memory

The relationships between these aspects of experience are what compose the human subject: perception and its relationships with affection and memory. One consequence of this configuration is that perception and affection are also matters of time: they can only be understood in terms of duration. Think of it this way: when I see a pin, past memories of pins are evoked, especially an understanding of the kind of pain associated with being pricked by a pin. Thus, my perception of a pin is inextricably linked with memories of other pins, and also to an affection associated with pins (the pain of being pricked by a pin). Therefore, any perception and any affection will always be intermingled with memories of the past.

There is a further issue here. If I have claimed that the subject for Bergson is a product of my body and the things my body comes into contact with, then it is also the case that one of the things my body comes into contact with is the past. This point requires further explanation. Perception and memory always go together to the degree that there can be no perception without memory. They do, however, constitute different "systems": perception is a different kind of thing than is memory—they are "different in kind," is the way Bergson puts it. In other words, we should not think of memories in terms of perception. It is incorrect to think, for example, that my memory of a pin is a sort of weak perception of a pin, as though memories are faded perceptions, that they are perceptions that have gone dim as a result of time. To do this latter would be to consider the difference between perception and memory as merely one of degree—a difference of degree—insofar as perceptions would be "strong" perceptions and memories would merely be "weak" perceptions. This is to conceive of the difference between them as one of quantity—that is, it is to conceive that memories merely have less of a quantity of perception than do perceptions per se. Rather, for Bergson, memories are qualitatively different from perceptions.

The relationship between perception and memory can therefore be seen as being somewhat analogous to the relationship between perception and affection, for like the perception-memory distinction, so too is the distinction between perception and affection a difference in kind, not of degree: affection is qualitatively different from perception; it belongs to a different "system," as it were. The way that all of this works can be brought together by way of a curious example from Bergson's *Matter and Memory*. Bergson states that "A certain time elapses before the child can touch with the finger the precise point where it has been pricked [by a pin]" (*MM*, 59). This is to say that the child has to "learn," in some sense, how affection is related to perception, how the feeling of pain "inside the body" is related to an object—the pricking of a pin—in the external world that is perceived. In short, the child will reach a point where its memory in the past of having seen and been pricked by a pin (or some such similar occurrence) can inform its apprehension of the relationship between an affection and a perception. Needless to say that this is a process that will be ongoing throughout one's life. We will always be experiencing new affections and perceptions and "learning" how to apprehend them, learning to know what such experiences feel like.

Affection is therefore related to memory. As I have already emphasized, the relationships between perception-affection and perception-memory are analogous, for each involves the relationship between an external factor—perception—and an internal one—affection or memory. What can be called the human "subject" is therefore composed of these factors, the combination of internal and external attributes; that is, the perceptions, affections, and memories of which the subject is composed. The comparison is striking insofar as this subject is composed of two factors that that seem to occur "inside" the subject—affections and memories. Perceptions, by contrast, are those things that seem to come to the subject from the "outside." But we must also conclude that these external factors are no less part of the subject than are the so-called internal factors, for we have claimed that perception and affection are intermingled no less than we have also claimed that perception and memory are interwoven. We will come to see that, as this book unfolds, Deleuze's conceptions of time and subjectivity will become even more complex than has been outlined here in relation to Bergson, but we have granted these notions of perception, affection, and memory a solid basis. Now we turn to the third great influence upon Deleuze who is essential for understanding his approach to cinema.

Deleuze and Philosophy: Spinoza

The third great influence on Deleuze is the seventeenth-century philosopher Baruch Spinoza. It may seem strange to call upon ideas proposed by a philosopher who was active nearly 400 years ago to theorize a medium that emerged in the late nineteenth century, but in conjunction with Nietzsche and Bergson, Spinoza provides a conceptual framework which enables Deleuze to flesh out his philosophy of cinema, especially as that philosophy articulates processes of subjectivity and subjectivization. As with the other philosophers approached here, there are three key concepts taken from Spinoza:

1 the body and affections
2 the spiritual automaton
3 passions and actions

Deleuze's 1968 book on Spinoza, *Expressionism in Philosophy*, foregrounds, among other things, Spinoza's bold claim that we do not yet know what a body can do.[20] Much of Spinoza's and Deleuze's argumentation on this point amounts to a refutation of Descartes's (1596–1650) prioritization of the mind at the expense of the body. As is well known, in his *Meditations*, Descartes begins from a position which asserts that the only thing I can be certain of—the only thing I can know for sure—is that I am a "thinking thing" (*res cogitans*), that "I think." Beyond this, I cannot even be certain my body exists, for I might merely *think* that it exists; it might merely be a fabrication of my mind. And nor can I be certain the external world exists—again, I might merely think it exists. In this way, for Descartes, the mind has a true existence in ways that render the existence of the body false—at any rate, the body has an existence of which I cannot be certain in the same way that I can be certain of the existence of my own thoughts.

Spinoza sets out to disprove Descartes's claims. He does this first of all by denying the mind any priority over the body. Rather, for Spinoza, the mind and the body are interrelated systems. There is an intrinsic correspondence between them, and neither has priority over the other. The key element here is Spinoza's conception of affection, and we will see that Spinoza's formulations on this point chime well with what we have already discovered in Bergson by way of affection. Like Bergson, for Spinoza affection is what occurs when one body comes into contact with another body or thing. What thereby results is what Spinoza terms "affection," by which he means that my body will suffer affects when another body touches it, and my mind will form an idea (or ideas) of this affection. Thus, the body and the mind operate together. What is central to Spinoza's philosophy, certainly as articulated in his *Ethics*, is the question of how my mind processes the affections that my body comes into contact with. To revert to an example we have already used at length, if I am pricked by a pin, how does the feeling or affection of this prick become something I can think or understand? In very simple terms, what is at stake here is the question of how I get from the feeling of being pricked by a pin to the realization that "I have been pricked by a pin," that is, to a comprehension of the fact that this pain in my arm has been caused by the pricking of a pin.

In setting out his philosophy in this way, Spinoza immediately pursues a direction that is contrary to that of Descartes. First of all, Spinoza conceives of the body and the mind as working in tandem. That which affects the body also affects the mind. Furthermore, the ways in which the body and the mind operate are interrelated. In many ways, for Spinoza the body has a certain priority over the mind insofar as thoughts are only secondarily derived from the affections experienced by the body. But as we will also see, in some ways the mind develops a certain advantage over the body too, for it is by way of the mind—though always working in concert with the body—that passive affections received by the body can be turned into active affections of which the mind can form clear conceptions. As Spinoza puts it, "An emotion which is a passion ceases to be a passion as soon as we form a clear and distinct idea of it."[21] Additionally, in what is a second point against Descartes, because affections originate in the external world—I cannot be affected by a pin unless that pin exists in the external world—then so too is Descartes's doubt about the existence of the external world rendered null and void.

Spinoza's notion of the *spiritual automaton* is also a response to Descartes's prioritization of the mind. Descartes's notion of the mind accepts that we can only prove that thoughts exist in the mind. Concrete, material objects may well not exist at all, or other human beings or animals, for that matter (except that, for Descartes, God would not dare deceive us in such a way).

The only things I can be certain of are the forms of things—as images or representations—that are "in" my mind. Such is Descartes's fundamental position. Against such conceptions, Spinoza argues that ideas are material. Ideas are not mere forms or representations, they are concrete, material things. If we conceive of this in terms of being pricked by a pin, then the material content of the idea is the pin as such, as well as the contact it makes with my body. These materials—skin and pin—form part of the idea, and conversely, the idea that is "in my head" is intimately connected with that material. The connection between form and content, or mind and body—or soul and body—is what Spinoza refers to as a "spiritual automaton." Thus, what we can call the human subject is not only a mind or thought, rather it is a combination of mind and body, of thought and matter. On the one hand, this conception offers a way of overcoming Descartes's prioritization of mind. On the other hand, we will also see how Deleuze comes to conceive of the cinematographic mechanism as a kind of spiritual automaton, as a mechanism capable of producing "material images," rather than mere representations or illusions. At any rate, the notion of a spiritual automaton is one that conceives of a combination of mind and body, or body and soul.[22]

A key objective of *Expressionism in Philosophy* is to account for the passage from *passive affections* to *active affections*. Spinoza, certainly in Deleuze's arguments, makes the quest to turn passivity into activity central to his philosophy. But he does this in a rather complex way. As Deleuze puts it, what is essential is finding ways in which passive affections can be turned into active affections. Being pricked by a pin offers a good example of a passive affection. It is something that happens to me—I am passive—and it is likely to cause me suffering or even sadness. In this way it decreases my capacity for happiness or joy. The best way to turn this passive affection into an active one is quite simply to avoid being pricked by pins! And yet, the way that this passage from passive to active occurs is not as simple as all that. First of all, undergoing the passive affection is crucial. If one does not expose oneself to such experiences, then one can never know what its pain or suffering is, and therefore, one will not be able to then transform such passive affections into something active and positive. In short, being subjected to passive affections can be a positive thing. Coming to understand that the pain in my arm has been caused by a pin is, or can be, a positive experience.

Certainly being pricked by a pin is a trite example. Nevertheless, it does introduce for us the three-step process which goes from passive to active affections insofar as Deleuze theorizes it. The first step concerns passive affections. What is a passive affection? A passive affection is one of which we have an inadequate idea. By this, Deleuze (and Spinoza) mean that we do not have a clear idea of what has caused this affection. Therefore, when I exclaim, "Ouch! What was that?" and grasp my arm where a pain has emerged, then this is an inadequate idea. I do not yet "know" that I have been pricked by a pin, and thus the affection is passive. Trying to discover what has caused the pain is the second step. To then bring such a pain under an adequate idea, and thus to potentially make it an active affection, is a matter of explaining its cause. Why is there a pain in my arm? Because I have been pricked by a pin. This is the third step.

There are further points to make. Understanding or explaining such a cause is a matter of what Spinoza calls common notions (and it is common notions that enable us to make the second step referred to above). Essentially this means that links must be made between things that have common properties; for example, I understand that what is common to pins is that they have a sharp point at one end, and that such points can quite easily puncture human skin. By way of such common notions I can therefore come to explain that the pain in my arm has been caused by the prick of a pin. Now, the passive affection of which I had only an inadequate idea has been turned into an affection of which I have an adequate idea: it is an active affection.

Not all passive affections involve pain and suffering. Indeed, the main aim of Spinoza's *Ethics* is to philosophize the ways in which pain and suffering can be reduced to a minimum. Thus, I can certainly be subjected to passive affections that I find very enjoyable, things that make me feel good and which increase my joy and happiness—say, the feeling of warm sunshine on my face. Deleuze calls these (via Spinoza) joyful passions, and in one of the great passages of *Expressionism in Philosophy*, explains the significance of those passions.

> A mind that forms an adequate *idea* is the adequate *cause* of the ideas that follow from it: this is the sense in which it is active. What, then, are the ideas that follow from the common notion which we form by the aid of joyful passions? Joyful passions are ideas of the affections produced by a body that agrees with our own; our mind by itself forms the idea of what is common to that body and our own; *from this flows the idea of an affection, a feeling, which is no longer passive, but active.* Such a feeling is no longer a passion, because it follows from an adequate idea in us; it is itself an adequate idea.[23]

Deleuze puts it exceptionally well by describing these joyful passions as those that occur when "a body agrees with our own," for it is the outcome of coming into contact with something that increases our feelings of happiness. One of the main aims of Spinoza's *Ethics* is to find the ways in which to increase and maximize our joyful passions and active affections, and also to decrease the passive affections that lead to sadness and suffering. To therefore form an adequate idea of what causes me happiness offers one way in which Spinoza places us on the path toward maximizing active affections. For example, I can form an adequate idea of the warm feeling of sunshine on my face insofar as it is a joyful passion, and I can then increase that passion in a way that makes it an active affection: I can expose myself to the sun's warming rays and, in doing so, I make that experience an active one.

What Is Perception?

We have now considered some of the philosophical influences which contributed to Deleuze's conceptions of cinema. But we are yet to bring these ideas to bear directly on the cinema itself. Much of the remainder of this book will be devoted to such a task. Before those steps can be taken, however, some further investigation of the specific traits of cinema, as theorized by Deleuze, must be taken into account. The key figure here is Bergson for, as I have already claimed, to a large degree the *Cinema* books are philosophical commentaries on Bergson.

I have already suggested that Bergson was in fact very critical of the cinematographic mechanism. He wrote his critique of cinema in 1908, in *Creative Evolution*, when cinema was only in its earliest years. But with this in mind, how does Deleuze somehow bring Bergson to cinema in a positive way? Let us begin with Bergson's critique. Essentially Bergson is critical of cinema because it is—in theory—composed of static images, immobile frames, and he equates this with the human tendency toward intellectualization and abstraction. He argues that the intellect always begins from immobility (*CE*, 171) and that the mind all-too often thinks abstractly, that it posits "a world that dies and is reborn at every instant" (*CE*, 26–7). In short, by being too intellectualizing and abstract, the human mind typically works in the same way that the cinematograph does: it breaks down real movement into immobile instants. On this basis, both human abstract thought and the cinematograph are rendered unreal, illusory, and abstract.

In many ways, Bergson's critique anticipates that made by Jean-Louis Baudry in his famous 1970 essay "The Ideological Effects of the Basic Cinematographic Apparatus." One element of Baudry's critique of the cinema apparatus was concerned with the nature of cinema projection. Writing of the process of projection, Baudry argued that "[t]he meaning effect produced does not depend only on the content of the images but also on the material procedures by which an illusion of continuity, dependent on the persistence of vision, is restored from discontinuous elements."[24] Baudry draws upon the common sense thesis on the persistence of vision by which static images when projected at an appropriate rate produce the illusion of movement. And for Baudry—as much as for Bergson's critique of the cinematograph—that is what such images are: illusions.

Deleuze sets about countering these kinds of arguments, claiming that "Even in his critique of the cinema Bergson was in agreement with it, to a far greater degree than he thought" (*C1*, 58). How does Deleuze go about making such an argument? He argues that it may well be the case that movement is made up of instants, just as a film is composed of separate cels or frames. But he argues that what is particular about film frames is that each single frame has the same value as any other single frame. No one frame is privileged as an instant as such. The result of this is that each individual frame exists only in relation to those near it. And insofar as this is the case, each frame is less a static frame than a frame that is in the process of moving: it is a frame that exists only in the context of its contributing to movement. In short, it makes no sense to conceive of the cinematographic cel as static, for it is always already in the process of being put into movement (see *C1*, 5).

Deleuze goes further than this. He tries to get to grips with Bergson's claims in *Creative Evolution*, that intellectual abstraction is a way of identifying the "outside of things," rather than experiencing them "from the inside." By making such abstractions we are thus recomposing the things of the world in an artificial way. Strikingly, and against cinema, Bergson claims that, by doing this, "we hardly do anything else than set going a kind of cinematograph inside us," and that "the mechanism of our ordinary knowledge is of a cinematographic kind" (*CE*, 332). Deleuze interprets Bergson's claims here in an interesting way, for he claims that Bergson's earlier book *Matter and Memory*, published in 1896, contains a much more convincing account of these kinds of processes. Yes, Bergson and Deleuze argue against intellectual abstraction. But Deleuze will claim that the cinematograph does not give us abstraction, and he uses Bergson's arguments from *Matter and Memory* in order to make his case. He does this in the following way—and I should warn readers that this is by no means straightforward.

Deleuze claims that, for Bergson, there is *no distinction between movement and image*. This, at first, seems like a very strange statement to make, for it seems entirely logical that movement and images are completely different sorts of things. So why would Deleuze—or Bergson—argue that these things can be considered, in some sense, as the same sorts of things? The reason is that each of these philosophers wants to bring into question the distinction between movement as something that occurs in the external world by way of objects, on the one hand, and images as things that occur in the mind, on the other. Thus, we typically tend to think that when I see a car moving, that the car itself is moving in the external world, while inside my mind there is a little image of a car, as though my mind is capable of producing these little interior images of external things. It is this distinction that Deleuze and Bergson wish to undo, specifically that our thoughts and experiences of the world are things that are computed or calculated by the mind in ways that are separate from the kinds of operations—movements—that occur in the external world. Deleuze and Bergson instead want to claim that these internal and external operations are connected: they are not separate. In some ways it is a matter of saying that the movements of the external world happen inside us, and, conversely, that our thoughts of things are also in the external world. As Bergson puts it at one point, "Perception, in its pure state, is, then, in very truth, a part of things" (*MM*, 64). At this point we can see Bergson's position as being somewhat similar to that of Spinoza in his critique of Descartes, for what Bergson seems to imply is precisely what Spinoza calls a spiritual automaton. Bergson is here breaking down the distinction between an internal mind, on the one hand, and the external world, on the other. What Bergson is, in fact, proposing is a radical relationship between mind and world in which mind and world are similar substances. In short, thinking—what Bergson articulates in terms of "images"—and movement are things than need not be opposed. The internal world of the human mind need not be opposed to or even be distinct from the external world of objects and things which lie outside us.

Images Are Not Representations of Things (Against Phenomenology)

There are profound consequences for this theorizing. One consequence is that *images are not representations of things*. Rather, images are things: images are not separate from the things that they are. There is not an image of a thing, on the one hand, and the thing (the so-called real thing), on the other. Rather, the image of the thing *is* the thing; it *is* the "real thing." When I see a car moving, then such an experience is not a matter of *a car moving in the external world* to which can then be added *an image of a car moving which is implanted in my mind*. Rather, the process of my perceiving a moving car is all there is: it is a moving car as perceived by me. This is a way of saying that there is no representation of a car "inside my mind," but that my mind is inseparable from the car it perceives. A perception of the car, for all intents and purposes, *is* the car.

Deleuze makes these arguments in order to clearly differentiate Bergson's position from that proposed by the philosophical movement known as phenomenology which emerged at much the same time as Bergson was writing. The chief exponents of phenomenology, certainly as singled out by Deleuze, were German philosopher Edmund Husserl (1859–1938) and French philosopher Maurice Merleau-Ponty (1908–61). Phenomenology begins from a perceived world that is all mixed up and in flux. We see things, but we do not quite know what to make of them. By way of what is known as the "phenomenological reduction," the phenomenological method then abstracts from the world-in-flux in order to arrive at fixed points which it can confidently determine. In other words, from an originating situation in which images and movements, mind and world, subjects and objects are all indeterminable and existing in processes of universal variation, phenomenology isolates and fixes upon constants, and those constants are, for the phenomenologists, reliable and repeatable. Indeed, such constants are those of a so-called natural perception, a mode of perceiving freed from the prejudices and distortions of subjective perception, such as the distortions of beliefs, customs, class, personal memory, or any other prejudice that might cloud a true or natural state of things. Such then is the phenomenological reduction and its appeal to "natural perception."

We can begin to see how such a position is radically different from that offered by Bergson. A key starting point for phenomenology is that things in the external world come into our minds in ways that are typically clouded or distorted in some way. These things that come into our minds are "images," but only in the sense that those images are representations "in our minds" of external things: they are representations. For phenomenology, to make those images into something real or true, we need to refine those images in our minds in specific ways so as to separate what is true and natural from that which is false and therefore distorted or inaccurate. The true images are the ones that will most accurately match what is really outside in reality. The process is therefore one of teaching our minds to replicate—to represent—as accurately as possible what really occurs in the external world. Thus, for phenomenology, images in the mind are very clearly separated from movements and things in the external world. The task for phenomenology is to get those separate elements—mind and world, subject and object, image and movement—to match in ways that are accurate, natural, and true.

Bergson, contrary to phenomenology, has a very different conception of how perception works. Instead of pictures in the mind which try to match up with objects in the external world, Bergson argues that what is in my mind *is* what is in the external world, and what is in the external world *is* in my mind. They are interconnected, and one cannot exist without the other. That is all the world there is, and that is how I experience the world. That *is* the world. Bergson does not claim that such an account of perception is true or natural. Rather, any account of the true or natural would have to account for the myriad connections and composites that are possible and existing in the world. This is a way of saying that all perceptions will be different. The way in which I see that car move is different from the way that you see that car move. And the world itself is made up of all those interrelated and conflicting perceptions. The perspective of phenomenology is entirely different from this. Phenomenology would rather reduce all the possible perceptions of the car to a single, definitive, true, and natural perception, a perception that would be "true for all" in some way.

Phenomenology therefore remains a philosophy of the subject, if by "subject" one means a subject whose traits are supposed to be universal, predictable, and determinable. Such subjects will, by following the phenomenological method, arrive at judgments that can be designated universal and true. Bergson, on the contrary, does not have this kind of conception of subjectivity. Rather, he subscribes to a notion of universal variation. All perceptions are imbued with their own being, and those perceptions will be infinitely variable: mine will be different from yours, and from those of another, and another. Such is Bergson's conception of human subjectivity: that which is infinitely variable.

To reiterate: what Bergson calls an "image" is thus very different from what phenomenology (and most other philosophies) call an image. For Bergson, "image" refers to the connection between *an object in the world* and *the way I perceive that object in the world*. But even dividing these is in some sense incorrect. The whole point of Bergson's analysis is to demonstrate that the way in which I perceive an object *is* that object: there is no difference between being and being perceived. These again might seem like very contentious claims to make—that there is no difference between a thing and my perception of a thing—but this is precisely what Deleuze argues. "The thing and the perception of the thing are one and the same thing, one and the same image," he writes (*C1*, 63). Or, to repeat one of his claims to which I have already referred, as Bergson puts it in *Matter and Memory*, "Perception, in its pure state, is, then, in very truth, a part of things" (*MM*, 64). Deleuze highlights the difference between Bergson's approach and that of phenomenology in the following way. "What phenomenology sets up as a norm," writes Deleuze, "is 'natural perception' and its conditions. Now, these conditions are existential coordinates," Deleuze continues, "which define an 'anchoring' of the perceiving subject in the world, a being in the world, an opening to the world expressed in the famous 'all consciousness is consciousness of something'" (*C1*, 57) Thus, phenomenology posits consciousness as an "inside" which is separated from what exists "outside" consciousness. From that perspective, consciousness cannot come into contact with that outside. It can only process various versions of that outside, a "consciousness of . . ." which will always remain separated from that which it is a consciousness of. Deleuze then argues that Bergson's approach "is the complete opposite" (*C1*, 60). For Bergson, "all consciousness *is* something." Consciousness does not separate itself from what is "outside" consciousness. On the contrary, what is outside consciousness remains consciousness itself: "It is indistinguishable from the thing" (*C1*, 61).

Cinema: Perception-Image, Action-Image, Affection-Image

If I have spent a long time explaining Bergson's accounts of perception and the image then it has been for a good reason: it has profound consequences for Deleuze's approach to cinema. For Deleuze, cinema has a consciousness. It perceives the world in terms of "images." And these are not representations of the world. They are not "images of" the world. Rather, such images are the world: cinema's images are intimately connected with the world.

As we saw earlier, perceptions are reductions. For example, if I need to cross a road, my perceptions will be geared to that task. I will not perceive everything. I will perceive only those things that are necessary for me to cross the road. Thus, from the complex manifold of things in the world, perception reduces the complexity of things in order to focus on and isolate aspects of the world that are relevant for it. And isn't this precisely how the cinema works? Certainly this is what Deleuze argues. "It is an operation," he writes, "which is exactly described as framing: certain actions undergone are isolated by the frame" (*C1*, 62). Like human perception, the cinema isolates aspects of the world, frames them, focuses on them, in order to make them part of its world. And this is precisely how human perception works anyway: "We perceive the thing, minus that which does not interest us as a function of our needs" (*C1*, 63). In short, perception isolates those things that are important for us. And yet, this raises the question of what is important, what are "our needs?" Essentially those things that are important are things we are receptive to, and which, correspondingly, may provoke us to act. All of this is part of a process that Deleuze will come to define as the components of the movement-image: the perception-image, the action-image, and the affection-image.

The first of these, the perception-image, is defined by Deleuze in the following way.

If the cinema does not have natural subjective perception as its model, it is because the mobility of its centres and the variability of its framings always lead it to restore vast acentred and deframed zones. . . . From the point of view which occupies us for the moment, we go from total, objective perception which is indistinguishable from the thing to a subjective perception which is distinguished from it by simple elimination or subtraction. It is this unicentred subjective perception that is called perception strictly speaking. And it is the first avatar of the movement-image: when it is related to a centre of indetermination it becomes a *perception-image*. (*C1*, 64)

Perception-image therefore means the way cinema perceives, and the way cinema perceives is essentially the ways in which it presents its images and sounds. Deleuze's definition might appear vague, but for the notion of the perception-image we must bear in mind all of the contours Deleuze brings, via Bergson to perception and to the image.

Much of this we have framed in terms of Bergson's difference from phenomenology. But there is another way to consider the perception-image, a way that should be fairly straightforward. We are very accustomed when talking about films to describing a film's images in terms of what they represent. A film set in Los Angeles will, in some way, be a representation of that city. Films featuring female characters, such as those directed by Max Ophuls, can be said to offer representations of women. Even more generally, film is said to capture reality, and by doing so it offers us representations of reality. Deleuze rejects this kind of characterization of cinema, for conceiving of cinema in terms of its ability to "represent reality" sets up an unnecessarily negative paradigm. From such a perspective, cinema will always be measured or judged by how well or poorly it "represents." Does it represent the world accurately? Does it represent women in a truthful or positive way? Does it offer a faithful representation of Los Angeles? And so on. From such a perspective, cinema and films will typically be defined by the ways in which they fall short of truth and reality. Indeed, from such a perspective, films and cinema will mostly be fated to never being able to truly represent reality, because, after all, they can only offer "representations" of reality, never reality itself. Deleuze rejects this by declaring that the images presented by films and cinema *are* reality: so there is no need to be constantly criticizing films for being inaccurate or misleading or untruthful. They are none of those things. Rather, they are as real as any other "image" offered to us by the world. Deleuze therefore concentrates on what films present, not what they may or may not *re*present. Questions of the truth or accuracy of a film's images are therefore not real problems for Deleuze. They are false problems, problems which cannot be answered. In taking such a position, Deleuze goes against many of the major trends in theorizing film.[25]

If this is the case for Deleuze, then, if it is not representations that are on screen when we see a film, what is it that is on screen when we see a film? Deleuze's answer is simply that what we see and hear on screen are not representations: they are perception-images. What he means to point to is that there is no division between cinema's images, on the one hand, and a real world, on the other. Cinema's images are part of the world, not distinct from it, not less than it, but part of it. And this is why Deleuze will claim that cinema has a consciousness. Much like human consciousness, what is internal to cinema— the images and sounds projected on screen—is also part of the external world, connected with that world, not separated from it in a lesser or secondary realm. We can defer to the Bergsonian claim that "consciousness *is* something," and not that "consciousness is consciousness *of* something," for so too can we say that "a film *is* something" rather than claiming that "a film is a film *of* something."

The perception-image, for all intents and purposes, is a reduction or "cutting out" of the world—we have seen such formulations from Bergson and Deleuze earlier. Its purpose is to give rise to action, and that is why the perception-image arises "as a function of our needs." To isolate a part of the world via perception is to isolate it in terms of the possibility of our acting on the world. When I see a car moving, then perhaps that perception is a function of my intention to cross the road: an action, no less. Deleuze puts it this way: "[P]erceiving things where they are, I grasp the 'virtual action' they have on me, and simultaneously the 'possible action' that I have on them, in order to associate me with them or to avoid them" (*C1*, 64–5).

To perceive is therefore a function of the capacity to act, and action is a normal or typical consequence of perception. Such actions, insofar as they pertain to cinema, form the second aspect of the movement-image: the action-image. The perception-action system forms something of a circuit. I perceive in order to act, and actions are the consequences of my perceptions. As Deleuze puts it, this circuit is a matter of "the virtual action of things on us and our possible action on things" (*C1*, 65). Thus, when I see there is no car coming along the road, I cross the road: that is my action. We shall come to understand later precisely how such actions function as examples of the action-image in cinema.

Before we can get to that point, however, there is a third major sub-regime of the movement-image: the affection-image. We have already come across Bergson's conception of affect or affection, for an affect is the product of one body's intersection with another body (or an object's intersection with another object or body). We saw such an occurrence in the example of "being pricked by a pin" from Bergson's *Matter and Memory*. Deleuze is quite clear here: affection is what occurs in between a perception and an action. When I am pricked by a pin, there is a delay—an "in-between"—that occurs between my perception-reception of the prick and my response or action which results from being pricked. The action—say, my clutching at my arm where the pin has entered my skin—will occur only after a delay, however brief or long. The delay, and in this example we can name that delay as "pain," is affection. Much the same then goes for what Deleuze then calls the affection-image.

> There is an in-between. Affection is what occupies the interval, what occupies it without filling it in or filling it up. It surges in the centre of indetermination, that is to say the subject, between a perception which is troubling in certain respects and a hesitant action. It is a coincidence of subject and object, or the way in which the subject perceives itself, or rather experiences itself or feels itself "from the inside." (*C1*, 65)

Between the cinema's processes of perception and action there occurs a delay, and that delay is the affection-image. As we saw earlier, the perception-action system in Bergson functions like an exchange. Between the perceptions received from the world and the action that is then exerted on the world, there arises an in-between, a delay between reception and action. If we conceive of this in terms of our crossing the road, then it functions here as something of a hesitation: when the road is clear, then I can make the decision to cross the road. And yet, this is not a particularly evocative example of affection. The pin prick will provide a better example, for it is precisely the delay between the reception of the pin's prick—*ouch!*—and my response to that occurrence—*I place my hand against the point on my arm where I have been pricked in an attempt to mask the pain*—that is affection. And the affective nature of that affection is, in this example, quite clear: it is *pain*.

The Material Aspects of Subjectivity

Across his definitions of the perception-image, action-image, and affection-image, Deleuze includes some discussion of what he calls the "material aspects of subjectivity." First of all, Deleuze claims that, for the perception-image, the material aspect of subjectivity is "subtractive" (*C1*, 63). And we have already seen the ways in which Bergson and Deleuze theorize perception in terms of that which is isolated according to our needs—in other words, we "subtract" from the world what interests us. The first material aspect of subjectivity therefore consists of a circuit between subject and world, a back-and-forth between subject and object, by means of which perceptions are grounded in the external world in accordance with our needs and interests.

The second material aspect of subjectivity pertains to action. Deleuze is very specific about its character. "[A]ction relates movements to 'acts,'" he writes, "which will be the design for an assumed end or result" (C1, 65). This formulation is key for conceiving of the movement-image, for, as we have seen, an action such as crossing a road is driven by need to achieve a result; that is, getting to the other side of the road. In simple terms, an action is geared toward an aim or result, and the action-image in the cinema is driven in much the same way. As we will see, the action-image can work on a large scale—for example, across the entirety of a film in terms of a "result" or ending to a film: the criminal is captured in the end, or the romantic couple is united so as to live happily ever after, and so on. Or such actions might lead to small scale results; for example, a character temporarily manages to escape his pursuers, or young lovers arrange a secret rendezvous, and so on. The key trait of this second material aspect of subjectivity is the calculation of *where I am now* in relation to *where I want to be*; that is, a calculation of what action must be performed in order to achieve a desired result.

The third material aspect of subjectivity pertains to the affection-image. As Deleuze initially puts it, this aspect concerns the way the subject feels itself "from the inside" (C1, 65). However, he goes into much more detail than this. What precisely occurs during these moments of affection? That is, what occurs during these moments that are comprised of a delay between a perception and an action, on the one hand, while, on the other hand, we have also called affection the conjunction between one body or thing and another body or thing? How can we make sense of all this? To clarify what is at stake for the affection-image, Deleuze isolates one particular aspect of human anatomy which gives special precedence to affection: the human face. Deleuze writes, "There is inevitably a part of external movements that we 'absorb,' that we refract, and which does not transform itself into either objects of perception or acts of the subject, rather they mark the coincidence of subject and object in a pure quality" (C1, 65). He continues, now more specifically describing the importance of the human face, arguing that, "For we, living matter or centres of indetermination, have specialised one of our facets, or certain of our points into receptive organs at the price of condemning them to immobility . . . . This is the origin," Deleuze continues, "of Bergson's wonderful definition of affection as 'a kind of motor tendency on a sensible nerve,' that is, a motor effort on an immbolised receptive plate" (*C1*, 65–6; cf *MM*, 55–6). Affection, then, is a delay between perception and action whose material aspect involves contact between one body or thing and another body or thing. But Deleuze notes in the quotation earlier that the human face—an "immobilized receptive plate"—occupies a particular focus of affections. Affections are "registered," as it were, on the human face. Thus, when I am pricked by a pin, it is highly likely that I will wince with the pain so that the features of my face become scrunched up, my eyes closed, my mouth agape. These responses are not actions—as I have said previously, an action here would be something like the subsequent placing of my hand upon the area where the pin has pricked my skin. But the affection will arise prior to the action. Affection is the pain that emerges in the delay between the perception of the pricking of the skin and the action which then responds to the affective pain. The face will often be a place of the human anatomy upon which a registering of the affection will occur, a place that is immobilized, by contrast with the arm or hand which is mobile and performs an action. The face, therefore, occupies a special place in Deleuze's notion of the affection-image.

Letter from an Unknown Woman

We have thus outlined specific aspects of the perception-image, action-image, and affection-image. We need to get back to a closer discussion of some cinematic examples. In this instance, I am going to look rather closely at one of Ophuls's Hollywood films, *Letter from an Unknown Woman*, released in 1948. I am going to argue that *Letter from an Unknown Woman* is an example of a movement-image. Therefore, I want to begin by asking a key question: what is a perception-image? I have already claimed that a perception-image is what the camera sees and hears. Correlatively it designates the sounds and images the cinema projector makes and shows. And yet, such a definition is surely far too general, so we must consider that the camera—or the film, to be precise—always chooses specific things to see and hear, and that it does so in very particular ways. So let us take *Letter from and Unknown Woman* as an example. Most of the film, like *La signora di tutti*, is told as a flashback, or series of flashbacks. The flashbacks are guided by the letter indicated in the film's title. Many of the flashbacks are narrated by the voice of the "unknown woman" also signaled in the film's title. Therefore, a first question to ask of the perception-images of this film is: what status do they have as images? As flashbacks, can we call them memory images, and if so, are they the subjective memories of a specific person—of the "unknown woman"—or might the film's images be ones that are more objective rather than merely subjective? What this all means is that determining precisely what a perception-image is in this context is by no means a straightforward task.

Let us take a closer look at *Letter from an Unknown Woman*. The film was not a great success upon its release in 1948. It has nevertheless become one of the most important examples of film melodrama and a crucial text for the study of women in classical Hollywood film, especially from a feminist perspective. Certainly, for Anglo-American film scholars, *Letter* stands as Ophuls's most important film, although it is not one to which Deleuze refers—indeed, Deleuze refers to none of Ophuls's American films. The story focuses on the life experiences of Lisa Berndle (Joan Fontaine) who, throughout her life, remains devoted to one man, a concert pianist named Stefan Brand (Louis Jourdan). There are several occasions during the film when Lisa and Stefan spend time together. These periods are enjoyably and passionately romantic. And yet, these meetings seem to be quickly forgotten by Stefan. For most of the film Lisa effectively remains an "unknown woman" to him—hence the film's title. *Letter* therefore offers something like a quintessential example of melodrama or of the classic "woman's film": a devoted woman who is shunned by the man she loves.

The film is set in Vienna around the year 1900 (so too is Ophuls's *La Ronde* set in the same time and place). It begins with Stefan returning to his apartment late one night with the news that he has been challenged to a duel at sunrise, a duel he will almost certainly lose. As a consequence, he asks his butler, John (Art Smith), to pack his things: he is going to flee rather than face his fate. John is mute, so without words, he hands Stefan a letter that had arrived that day. Stefan sits down to read it. We also read the opening lines of the letter as they appear to us on screen—rather like the letter which closes *La signora di tutti*. At the same time a woman's voiceover begins to recite those lines for us. This is the woman we will come to know as Lisa, and those opening lines tell us, "By the time you read this I may be dead." On the basis of this, the film now drifts back, by way of flashback, to Lisa's youth, to the time when she first encountered Stefan as he was having his household belongings moved to an apartment in the same building where Lisa lived with her widowed mother. It happens that Stefan is a concert pianist with great promise, and Lisa falls in love with him immediately. Her voiceover tells us that, from the moment they set eyes upon each other, she began to quite consciously "prepare" herself for him. And that first moment he sees her, "notices" her, is dramatically staged. One day she catches him leaving the apartment building and opens the door for him. It is a glass door and she opens it back upon herself so that, as Stefan walks past, she sees him through the door, and yet is also shielded from him by the door. Ophuls then gives us a point-of-view shot from Stefan as he thanks Lisa. Following this encounter, in "preparing" herself for him, Lisa begins to take extra care of her appearance and clothing. She reads up on the great musicians, attends dancing classes so as to become more graceful, and so on. One day she manages to sneak into Stefan's apartment. She glides up to his piano, the piano she has so often heard him play as she has listened outside his apartment window. John (Stefan's butler) sees her in the apartment. He is sympathetic and understands Lisa's motivations.

And then comes the crushing news that Lisa's mother is to remarry and that they will relocate to the town of Linz. Lisa is going to be taken away from the love of her life. On the day of their move, Lisa runs away from the railway station shortly before their train is due to leave, for she cannot bear to be parted from Stefan. She returns to the apartment block and rushes up the stairs only to discover that Stefan is not there. She waits for him until finally he returns—with another woman on his arm! They disappear into his apartment, and Lisa disappears to Linz with her voiceover declaring, "There was nothing left for me."

In Linz, now eighteen, Lisa has been set up with an eligible young lieutenant who is otherwise insufferably boring and conventional. When he asks her for her hand in marriage, she quite fraudulently declares that she's already engaged. Her declaration causes a scandal, her reputation is ruined, and Lisa returns to Vienna. She finds work as a model in a women's clothes store where every night after work she waits across from the entrance to Stefan's apartment in the hope of meeting him again. One night, he does notice her, suggesting "I've seen you before," with a puzzled look on his face. They spend the evening together. He takes her to dinner and he's flattered by her interest in him. A standout episode of the evening is their visit to the Prater Amusement Park where they ride in a faux train which enables them to "travel" to exotic places—Venice, Switzerland, and so on—by way of a series of moving screens. As they are enjoying this amusement, Lisa tells Stefan of the imaginary travels she took with her father as a child. Later they go to a café and dance arm in arm. They return to his apartment and she enters in the same manner as she had seen another woman do some years before.

The next day Stefan finds her working at the clothes store. He tells her that he must leave immediately for Milan, to play at La Scala, no less. He has become a famous concert pianist. She sees him off at the railway station where he states that he'll be back in two weeks. But Lisa knows better than this. "Two weeks," her voiceover declares. "Stefan, how little you knew yourself," she continues. "That train was taking you out of my life."

And it does. That scene dissolves to reveal Lisa being cared for at a convent where she has just given birth to a baby boy whom she comes to name Stefan. Against the wishes of the nuns at the convent who have cared for her, she refuses to state who the father is. The film's images here switch back to Stefan reading the letter. We see that Lisa has included some photographs of the young Stefan with her letter.

Some years later, when young Stefan is nine years old, we see that Lisa has married Johann Stauffer (Marcel Journet). It is a marriage of convenience to a man who knows her troubled history. One evening, to celebrate Lisa's birthday, the married couple attends a performance of *The Magic Flute*. At this performance Lisa, after many years, once again encounters Stefan. We hear from the chatter of other operagoers that Stefan's career has foundered. He is considered a failure whose promise went unfulfilled. But Lisa is once again besotted. Her passion for Stefan overtakes her, and she feels she must return home. As she is waiting in the foyer of the opera house for her carriage, Stefan appears. He again fails to recognize her, though he is struck by the impression that he has seen her somewhere before. "Who are you?" he asks. He tries to fathom where he has seen her before. She must leave, but he asks if he can see her again. Lisa can give him no guarantee. When she gets into her carriage, her husband is there. He warns her against meeting with Stefan again. "There are such things as honor and decency," he argues, telling Lisa that she has a will of her own. But she replies that she has never had any will but Stefan's: she simply cannot help herself.

In order to arrange a rendezvous with Stefan, Lisa arranges for her son to travel to the country for two weeks. In a scene that repeats her earlier farewell of Stefan for two weeks, she farewells her son from a train compartment just as a train guard tells them that they cannot remain in this compartment:

it was to have been quarantined. We later hear that there had been a case of typhus on board. Lisa meets Stefan that evening, unaware that her husband has followed her. While gesturing toward a small statue in his apartment, Stefan tells of a statue made by the ancient Greeks for a god they did not know, but who they hoped one day would come. Stefan reckons he has done much the same with the statue he has. He has hoped every day that a goddess would appear to him that would bring about the fulfillment of his dreams, but now he has reached the point where he knows that this day will never come. Lisa, of course, is crushed by this admission, aware that she will never be Stefan's goddess. After this, Stefan chatters idly, as though Lisa means little to him other than a brief dalliance. Lisa now knows she will remain forever "unknown" to him. He will never want her in the way she wants him. Her voiceover tells us that she had come here this night in order to give Stefan her whole life, "but you didn't even remember me," she says. And so she leaves, passing the butler, John, on the stairs as she departs. Outside, a man on the street mistakes her for a prostitute (a nod, perhaps, to the episodes of *La Ronde*).

We next hear that her son has died of typhus, and that Lisa, too, has died. We reach the final lines of her letter. As Stefan reads these lines, images of Lisa flash before us, images we have seen before in this film we have been watching, and it is supposed that these must be images that are flashing through Stefan's mind, as though it is only now that he is finally remembering Lisa. He buries his head in his hands, presumably distraught at the life he has damaged. He asks his butler if he remembers this woman, and he does indeed. He writes the name "Lisa Berndle" for Stefan.

Stefan then hears a carriage arrive outside his window. It is time for the duel. It appears that Stefan has decided to face his fate after all. It is also presumed that the duel is with Johann Stauffer as a matter of protecting the latter's "honor and decency." We hear some parting voiceover words to Stefan from Lisa. "If only you could've recognized what was always yours, what you'd never lost." Stefan smiles as he gets into his carriage, just after he has seen an evocation or memory-image of Lisa as a young girl standing at the front door of the apartment complex, a reminder of the very first time he had set eyes upon her.

Such, then, is the action of *Letter from an Unknown Woman*. And yet, the question remains as to what a "perception-image" might mean here. We know that, for Deleuze and Bergson, perception isolates aspects of the world as a function of our needs, so a perception-image in the cinema will always be related to what is achieved by that which is seen and heard. Therefore, any perception-image will be related to action, and a key question for the perception-image will be: what does a film achieve, especially by way of its action? As we will hopefully know by now, for Deleuze, actions are movements designed to achieve a result. A first way, therefore, to consider this film's perceptions is by way of Lisa and her actions, for it is primarily by way of her flashbacks and narration that we arrive at this film's achievement. As one commentator puts it, we never see Lisa as others see her, for we only ever see Lisa as she sees herself.[26] Much the same could be said for the other characters: it is only ever through Lisa's eyes that we see Stefan, or Lisa's mother, son, husband, and so on. Nevertheless, there may well be important moments that are not dictated by Lisa's perceptions, with the film's opening and closing sequences being prime examples, for these are scenes that occur after Lisa's death. And yet, some commentators will declare that Lisa had intended such outcomes anyway, that Stefan's departure for the duel and certain death are in some way Lisa's intended revenge upon him for his failure, until the very last, to remember and recognize her.[27]

Let us have a closer look at this possibility. Consider that, right near the film's end, Ophuls offers us a meticulous, carefully framed scene in which Lisa arrives outside Stefan's apartment. Lisa is filmed here from what appears to be a strangely distant perspective from a long way down the street on which the apartment building is located. Lisa enters the building, and then the camera pans an elaborate 180° in order to reveal that we have in fact been watching Lisa from roughly the same position as her husband, for he is shown to us in his carriage where he has been watching Lisa enter Stefan's apartment building. And thus we might be entitled to declare that here is a scene that is not perceived from Lisa's perspective. And yet, on the other hand, one might argue that Lisa has deliberately engineered this confrontation so that the duel between Stefan and her husband is, in fact, a consequence Lisa fully intends. This point is one that is explored in greater detail later.

Now, it is on points such as these that any account of *Letter from an Unknown Woman* becomes rather complicated. We need to ask: what is achieved by this film? It is only then that we will be able to identify the contours of the action-image in the film, and thus be able to locate the guiding thread of a perception-image. (Later, too, we will be able to define this film's affection-images.)

A Feminist Reading

One approach to the film argues that Stefan, not Lisa, is *Letter*'s central character. Thus, while Lisa offers the drama and emotional ups and downs of the film, it is ultimately by way of Stefan that the film achieves its moral lesson. He concedes to fate at the film's end. He gives up his superficial life and its shallow romantic dalliances so as to finally confront life in all its depth and gravity. He will "face the music," as it were, and attend the duel. The film's lesson therefore might be something along the lines of "Life is serious, and those who fail to take it seriously can irreparably damage those who are victims of their frivolity. To live a true life one must be serious and be aware of the consequences of one's actions." Less prosaically this kind of interpretation can be considered from the perspective of a feminist critique of *Letter*, for it is on the basis of the sacrifice of the woman that the man comes to discover a sense of truth and goodness. Lisa has devoted herself to Stefan, and it is on the basis of this devotion that Stefan finally achieves a sense of self-recognition, a true sense of "who he is." And thus the film's underlying lesson for women—a negative one from a feminist perspective—is that they should sacrifice themselves to men for the sake of the betterment of men. A strong feminist critique of the film will therefore consider that it demonstrates the general suppression of women by men.[28] Lisa's sacrifices for and devotion to Stefan thus show us what he could have had all along. They show us that the goddess he was searching for was there right in front of him, and that it was Lisa's face, after all, that could bring him satisfaction and happiness: this is what he comes to realize at the film's end. Thus, the film's lesson is that men should be grateful for the love bestowed upon them by selfless women. Of the moments of life Lisa shared with Stefan and their child, Lisa's voiceover tells us right near the end of the film, as though speaking directly to Stefan, "if only you could've shared those moments, if only you could've recognized what was always yours."

What *Letter from an Unknown Woman* therefore shows us is Stefan's self-delusion, and what it achieves is a certain shattering of this delusion, a "coming to his senses," at the film's end. Insofar as the film's images would be ordered in accordance with this result—as we have seen Deleuze claim, actions are movements designed to achieve a result—if the result is a matter of Stefan's self-discovery, then that will be what the film's perception-images are directed toward: Lisa's devotion, Stefan's profligacy, all culminating in his self-realization. From such a perspective, then, *Letter from an Unknown Woman* is a film about the struggles of men.

A Tale of Masochism

I suspect that such a reading of *Letter* will satisfy few people, and I would certainly have difficulty believing Deleuze would endorse such a reading. I think we need to believe that this is, in fact, a "woman's film," to the degree that it is a film whose central character is a woman. Thus, another possible interpretation sees the film as a deliberate triumph of masochism for Lisa. Masochism, on a dictionary definition, is a tendency to take pleasure from one's own suffering. This kind of interpretation reckons that Lisa deliberately makes her love for Stefan an impossible love, for it is only by being kept at a distance, as a fantasy or illusion, that this love can then be idealized. Gaylyn Studlar, who has convincingly argued along these lines, uses some of Deleuze's writings on masochism to support her arguments. She claims that the system the film puts in place is a fantasy-based one, and that it is the masochist, Lisa, who controls the fantasy. Therefore, Lisa is not at all a passive victim in the film. Rather, she is the controller of events. Studlar argues, for example, that Lisa effectively controls Stefan. It is she who seduces him and seeks him out. It is certainly not he who seduces her. At all times, Studlar additionally claims, Lisa keeps Stefan at the "right" distance. She does not want him to be too close to her, too intimately connected, for such a close connection could entail a sense of the loss of her selfhood. To be too close to Stefan would result in her losing control of the relationship between them which she has so carefully constructed. In other words, Lisa is a masochist, and she does not desire a "normal" romantic relationship. "Lisa's search is not for normal object love with its demands for mutuality and intimacy," writes Studlar.[29] Thus, the seeming failure of her romance with Stefan is, in fact, a triumph. Things turn out for Lisa in precisely the way she wants them to, and this satisfies her masochistic desire.

Deleuze himself writes of such motivations in relation to masochism. He argues that "What we need to do," if we are masochists, "is to 'put on wings' and escape into the world of dreams." The masochist, he continues, "does not believe in negating or destroying the world, nor in idealizing it: what he does is to disavow and thus to suspend it, in order to secure an ideal which is itself suspended in fantasy." Finally, Deleuze then states that the masochist "questions the validity of existing reality in order to create a pure ideal reality."[30] On the basis of Deleuze's claims here, we could argue that this is precisely the kind of "ideal reality" that Lisa creates for herself, not one that really exists, but one that is suspended in fantasy, a fantasy-love Lisa maintains for Stefan. Even the periods of their separation—sometimes for many years—fuel this fantasy. Indeed, Deleuze argues that the pleasure of waiting is essential to the masochistic fantasy.[31]

Near the end of the film, therefore, when Lisa claims that she has no will of her own, that her will has always been Stefan's, then on the one hand she is deceiving herself, for from a masochistic perspective she has always been in control of this scenario. On the other hand, however, she is correct, for it is her masochistic perversion—her "unconscious"—that is controlling her. At any rate, this is what Studlar argues by conceiving of *Letter from an Unknown Woman* in terms of Deleuze's account of masochism. The end of the film is therefore a triumph for Lisa. Studlar puts it this way: "Lisa's omnipotent control over events is magically reasserted in the masochistic triumph that reaches 'beyond the grave': she successfully alters the course of Stefan's life as her letter moves him to 'choose' noble death in a duel with her husband."[32]

What is the perception-image here? It can only be one that Lisa controls. She is a "master of ceremonies" carefully organizing her own romantic attachments, perhaps in the manner of the MC from *La Ronde*. And the film's action—its action-image—is therefore one that maintains Lisa's pleasurable masochism, and the film shows us the triumph of that pleasure.

Another Reading: George M. Wilson

And yet, is this really what *Letter from an Unknown Woman* is about? I find it difficult to come away from this film without seeing it as anything other than a tragic tale of lost love in which both of the central characters meet their deaths. How can that be a triumph of pleasure, masochistic, or otherwise? (Though, as we shall see, a Deleuzian take on these issues will see it as not necessarily tragic.) Another strong reading of the film, one which certainly does not see the film in terms of the pleasurable triumph of any of its characters, is offered by George M. Wilson. He argues that the film is concerned to show us two characters who are suffering from illusions of love, that not only the loves they seek are ideal and thus impossible, but also that this is what leads to the film's tragic ending. Lisa has idealized her love for Stefan, while Stefan is also beholden to an impossible ideal—hence his story of the Greek statue—to the degree that he is unable to recognize the potentially real-world devotion Lisa pays to him until it is too late.

Wilson argues that Lisa is "closed off" from her experience of the world. Her idealized fantasies overpower her capacity to foster a "real world" connection to the world and other human beings. And much the same case is made for Stefan. He whiles away his time in ways that are wasteful and admits that he's merely been waiting for something or someone special—a "goddess"—to rescue him from his life's failures. Wilson spends a good deal of time reflecting on Lisa and Stefan's ride on the imaginary train at the amusement park, for this symbolizes clearly their preference for imaginary worlds rather than the real world. "Both Lisa and Brand," he writes, "seem regularly on the verge of breaking through their private idealizations into some form of vivid awareness of the other," and yet, this never quite comes about.[33] And that is the film's tragedy: the characters' inabilities to come to know each other and themselves.

Wilson makes some excellent observations on Lisa's character. On the one hand, she is very much isolated, as though suffering from a lack of contact and understanding with other human beings—her friend on the swing early in the film, her mother, the lieutenant in Linz, the other women she works with at the dress store, her husband, and finally and primarily Stefan himself. But on the other hand, she is also very much an active force in the film: she holds the door open for Stefan at their first "meeting"; she steals into Stefan's apartment; she waits outside his apartment until he notices her; she refuses the offer of marriage from the lieutenant in Linz without flinching, while also knowing the damage it will do to her prospects; and she even takes the extraordinary step of leaving her husband so as to be with Stefan. These are all acts of extraordinary courage and daring, even though they are also acts which, from Wilson's perspective, exacerbate Lisa's illusory relationship to the world. This is never more pronounced for Wilson's arguments than when Lisa makes the decision to defy her husband's appeals for her to not arrange a rendezvous with Stefan. "Lisa's pursuit of Stefan Brand," he writes, "is a strict rejection of the convenient, the comfortable, and the ceremonial in personal relations. It is a rejection of the usual commerce of love," he adds.[34]

Yes, Lisa rejects the "usual commerce of love," but ultimately Wilson counts this against her. According to Wilson, she goes too far in the opposite direction. If the usual commerce of love represents a poor life choice, then it is still better than the crazy choice Lisa makes to return to Stefan (Wilson writes of "a certain craziness in Lisa").[35] It is Lisa's inability to provide realistic or reasonable boundaries to her imaginary fantasy of union with Stefan that precipitates the film's tragic conclusion. For Wilson, in short, Lisa, and women in general, should know better than to harbor such unrealistic fantasies.

Stanley Cavell on *Letter*

Wilson is a philosopher, and he is not the only philosopher to have attempted to untangle the challenges set by *Letter from an Unknown Woman*. For Stanley Cavell, the film is all about the ways in which Stefan fails to come to know Lisa—she is, for him, an "unknown woman"—and this is the film's tragedy. Cavell expands this theme to reflect on some general philosophical issues relating to skepticism, so that the film offers a general lesson on the difficulty of ever really knowing another human being. Such issues may be ones relating to gender too, for the film seems to give us the idea that it is particularly men who have difficulty coming to know or understand who women are, what they want or desire (whether this be Stefan, Johann, or the lieutenant in Linz).

But Cavell digs rather deeper than this. He reckons the film's themes might have something to say about Stefan's inability to achieve a fulfilled life, for Stefan wanders through life as though something of a ghost who is incapable of building a world for himself that would bring him satisfaction. In Nietzschean terms, Stefan fails to "become who he is"—and Cavell does invoke Nietzsche, even if his main philosophical inspiration is American philosopher Ralph Waldo Emerson.[36] Lisa offers Stefan a way out. She wants to rescue him, as it were. Throughout the film she wants to show him who he could be. At one point when talking to Stefan she tells him, "Well, I can't say it very well, but sometimes I felt when you were playing [the piano] that you haven't quite found what you were looking for." But there is surely more than this too. Lisa thinks that by entering Stefan's world she too might have the possibility to "become who *she* is." For Cavell, it is Lisa's quest for a better life, for a perfect life, that guides her actions, for it is worth her while to stake everything on her relationship with Stefan. It is in this way that she might find it possible to achieve a perfect life and "become who she is."

This amounts to a bold way of reading *Letter from an Unknown Woman*. In some ways it is difficult to see Lisa as a hero. On the contrary, there are many ways in which Lisa is depicted as passive, as a victim, and we are justified in believing at the end of the film she has lost everything, that her life has been a failure and that the one dream she staked her life on has not come true. And don't we get the impression that Lisa has in fact, even at the beginning of the film, given up on herself, and that her devotion to Stefan amounts to an erasure of herself?

Right near the beginning of the film she seems to make it clear. From the moment she sets eyes on him, she begins "quite consciously to prepare" herself for him, as though her own self did not matter, but that doing anything and everything to please Stefan is paramount. It can hardly come as a surprise when, near the end of the film, she makes the outrageous statement to her husband that she has never had a will of her own, that her will has always been Stefan's. Such admissions would seem to count entirely against the possibility that *Letter from an Unknown Woman* is about Lisa's Nietzschean quest to "become who she is." On the contrary, it seems more to be about erasing herself in the quest to be subject to Stefan. And even this quest fails, as we well know. But Cavell is prepared to give Lisa the benefit of the doubt. Amid the failures there are strivings toward triumph, for she is convinced that a life away from Stefan is not a life worth living, that she cannot bear to live with a dullard lieutenant in a provincial town, that her marriage to Stauffer is a marriage of convenience, not a marriage of fulfillment and enrichment. A life with Stefan does, on the contrary, hold such a promise, the promise of a life that will be worth living, and this is why Lisa will stake everything on it.[37]

In the end, Cavell's summation is a negative one. He argues that Lisa's quest for transcendence or betterment by way of her desire to be with Stefan is "morally debased."[38] Cavell thinks this because Lisa's quest is so much dependent on the whims of another person: Stefan. Her quest is not, to that extent, dependent on her self. It is less a matter of "becoming who she is" than a matter of negating her own existence in favor of another's. And that is not a triumph.

What Would Deleuze Say about *Letter from an Unknown Woman*?

Against Cavell and Wilson, might we instead see Lisa's life as a triumph? This is what I propose to do from a Deleuzian perspective. As a place to start, Deleuze would surely approve of Lisa's attempts to find a better life, to escape from conventional society so as to secure a world of her own on her own terms, something she believes Stefan will be able to provide for her. As Nietzsche puts it in his *Genealogy of Morality*, "We are unknown to ourselves. . . . We have never looked for ourselves."[39] It is by way of Stefan that Lisa "looks for herself." This motivation emerges early in the film by way of Lisa's desire to prepare herself for Stefan. She is entranced less by Stefan than by the world and life he represents, a world of culture and art that is far removed from the bourgeois conventionality that has marked her young life. Thus, much of the film shows us Lisa's attempts to transform this passive affection—her desire for Stefan—into an active one. She makes this transformation the goal of her life.

Alongside Lisa's quest to "become who she is" is a desire that she enter a world that will be worthy of her. Again, the Nietzschean aspects of Deleuze's philosophy can act as a guide, because discovering or creating a world for herself will require something like a "revaluation of all values." Lisa rejects the conventionalities expected of her. She tries to run away from her mother's remarriage to a military man in Linz. She also rejects a marriage proposal that by conventional standards would be considered a good match. Eventually she will even abandon the marriage that has delivered conventionality and the trappings of high society to her.

Lisa does all of this actively. These are decisions and acts she herself makes. Again, in Nietzschean terms, Lisa is active rather than reactive. By contrast, Stefan is utterly reactive. Lisa's actions take a rather particular form. Her striving for a better world assumes the form of a dream. *Letter from an Unknown Woman*'s closest cinematic relations might therefore be the films of Vincente Minnelli, on which Deleuze writes extensively in the *Cinema* books. In films such as *The Pirate* (1948), *The Band Wagon* (1953), or *Brigadoon* (1954), all of them musicals, a character, or characters, are trying to find their way from one world to another, from this world, with all of its inadequacies and compromises, to a better world. For Deleuze, this is the key question of Minnelli's films: "How, then, do we pass from one world to another?" (*C2*, 63). Deleuze's answer is that we do so by way of the dream. "[Minnelli's] work in musical comedy," Deleuze argues, "but also in all other genres, follows the obsessive theme of characters absorbed by their own dream, and above all by the dream of others and the past of others" (*C1*, 118–19). Although Deleuze is here writing of Minnelli's films, how better to conceive of *Letter*? This is a film in which Lisa is captivated by her own dream, but also that her dream is what she dreams for another person, that is, for Stefan. This is what *Letter* strives for: Lisa's attempts to go from one world to another, better world, a world that exists in her dreams and fantasies.

We can also claim that Lisa's desire for a better world is a consequence of the masochism that has often been attributed to her character. We have seen this expressed in Studlar's arguments, but Deleuze himself defines the masochistic scenario with tremendous force. The masochist has to "put on wings" and "escape into a world of dreams," he writes. In doing this, the masochist "questions the validity of existing reality" and in response creates "a pure ideal reality."[40] By way of her infatuation with Stefan, Lisa achieves all of this: a questioning of existing reality and its stultifying conventions, and the possibility of escape into "another world," a world of dreams that she can share with Stefan, even if only fleetingly. This escape into a world of dreams is nowhere better realized than in the train ride Lisa and Stefan share at the amusement park. As numerous commentators have pointed out, the scene demonstrates Lisa's preference for an imaginary world over the real one. The contrast between this imaginary train and the real ones that blot the course of Lisa's life is not subtle. One of those real trains signals her departure from Vienna for Linz, and therefore her separation from Stefan. Another shows us Stefan's severance from her, while a final train takes Lisa's son to his death, and it is presumed the same typhus virus from this train also takes Lisa's life. But we have to understand that the imaginary moments, the dream moments such as the ride on the amusement park train in which Lisa enters into the dream of another life, demonstrate to Lisa the possibility of escaping from the compromises and conventionalities of existing reality.

These gestures of getting out and of trying to discover or invent a better world amount to acts of what Deleuze called, when writing with Félix Guattari, lines of flight: the quest for a person or character to escape from existing reality into another reality.[41] A line of flight is something like an escape, but a distinction Deleuze and Guattari make is that between what they call "escape" and "a clean break." "Escape" implies a temporary going away, which thereby also implies that one will eventually return: the escape will only be short-lived. A clean break, on the other hand, is something you cannot come back from: a clean break establishes the terrain of a new world from which it will be impossible to return to the old world. As Deleuze states, "The line of flight is a deterritorialization."[42]

On these points Deleuze takes English novelist D. H. Lawrence as something of a guide, for it is Lawrence who wrote of the need to escape: "To get away, out of our life. To cross a horizon into another life. No matter what life, so long as it is another life," wrote Lawrence.[43] One way to conceive of this in *Letter from an Unknown Woman* is via the contrast between the light, white world of Linz and the dark, evening environments of Vienna. These are ways of conceiving of different worlds, and of the way that Lisa aspires to move from one world—the world of bourgeois conventionality—to another world, a new life. V. F. Perkins has written with great eloquence on these aspects of *Letter*, especially of how the scenes in Linz are full of glaring daylight that show us the starkness of the military world contained there, as well as washing out the significance of Lisa's face: she invariably wears white in Linz, and thus any radiance from her facial expressions is nullified. Even more than this, the scenes in Linz are set up so that they emphasize Lisa's containment or entrapment. She is often forced into corners, or framed by fences. Some of this kind of mise-en-scène is later repeated in the foyer of the opera house where Lisa's white clothing is once again swallowed up by the lavish white interiors. All of this emphasizes her concession to social convention and the stifling of her dreams and fantasies. But later, when she has left the opera performance and encounters Stefan, she is positioned in darkness all the more to enable her to glow for Stefan. And that glow is characteristic of all of the Vienna sequences when Lisa is with Stefan. Those scenes occur mostly at night, where Lisa's radiance comes to the fore. There, we are offered "[t]he presentation of Lisa's face as a globe," writes Perkins, "lit from within . . . to shine in the surrounding darkness."[44]

The film might therefore be conceived in terms of Lisa's aspirations to discover a "line of flight." If this is the case, we have good reason to conceive of *Letter from an Unknown Woman* as a great feminist text that opens up a vision of a better life that a woman can imagine, can dream. Thus, Lisa Berndle can be placed alongside other great heroines who dreamed of escape, alongside Emma Bovary in Gustave Flaubert's *Madame Bovary*, Nora in Henrik Ibsen's *A Doll's House*, Daisy Miller in Henry James's *Daisy Miller*, Clarissa Dalloway in Virginia Woolf's *Mrs Dalloway*, and others.[45]

We have seen that Lisa is active throughout *Letter*. She engineers her encounters with Stefan; she controls them. And yet, it would seem that at the end of the film she is defeated: she has left her husband; Stefan has barely managed to remember her; her son has died; and so too does Lisa die. And thus it would appear that, rather than being triumphantly active, Lisa ultimately succumbs to "passive affections," as Spinoza would call them: a broken heart, rejection, and isolation. Although numerous commentators view the film in such a way—we have certainly seen George M. Wilson and Stanley Cavell deliver such judgments—such a reading overlooks the final elements of the recited letter. Lisa's voice from beyond the grave tells us, as it also tells Stefan, that, "If this letter reaches you believe this: that I love you as I've always loved you. My life can be measured in the moments I've had with you and our child." There are regrets—she regrets that Stefan has been unable

to fully share those moments—but Lisa nevertheless reckons
that her life and her moments with Stefan have been worth
it, worth everything. To this degree, she does manage the task
of turning passive affections into active affections. From one
perspective, yes, the film's conclusion is tragic. But from another
perspective, it is the fulfillment of Lisa's desire, a best possible
outcome. It ensures that her love for Stefan can remain for her
as a dream, as an active triumph of her masochism, as though
this outcome was, in fact, what Lisa had always wanted. The
evocation of Nietzsche's notion of the "eternal return" in Lisa's
words—"My life can be measured by the moments I've had
with you"—is significant, for this amounts to a declaration
that it was all worth it, that Lisa's life has been worth it, that
her life would have been worthless without these moments,
and indeed that her life has been fulfilling because of those
moments. Thus, if all the moments of her life were to return to
her, she would gladly relive them, eternally, in accordance with
Nietzsche's conception of eternal return. As Nietzsche himself
puts it, "The question in each and every thing, 'Do you desire
this once more and innumerable times more?'" is one to which
Lisa can give an unreserved "yes."[46]

We can therefore declare that this is what *Letter from an
Unknown Woman* achieves. It shows us how Lisa "becomes
who she is." We might initially want to point out that *Letter* is
thus very different from *La signora di tutti*, for the latter film
is one in which the protagonist decides, in the end, that she has
failed, that her life choices have been mistaken, primarily that
her love affair with Leonardo did not bring her happiness, and
that she should have chosen Roberto. Lisa, contrary to this,
admits to no failure. Rather, she makes a series of best choices:
to renounce marriage with a dullard military man, to accept a
marriage of convenience with Stauffer, but then also to leave
Stauffer when the opportunity presents itself. Each step along
the way is an aspect of Lisa's becoming who she is. That is
what *Letter from an Unknown Woman* achieves.

From a Deleuzian perspective, key issues in *Letter* therefore
relate to what kind of perception-image occurs here, and

what kind of action-image? The action-image is determined by Lisa's actions. As argued earlier, the action-image might be considered from the total context of a film, or it might pertain to actions that occur in a scene or episode of a film. Most of the time it will be both of these, and that is the case in *Letter from an Unknown Woman*. Throughout the film, the action-image is shaped by Lisa's quest to become who she is, and that quest is brought to its fruition by the letter which enables Lisa to give expression to her life, and by Stefan's acceptance of his fate. But it is the series of small actions which build toward this conclusion that are the definitive actions of the film: Lisa's first encounters with Stefan, her listening to his piano playing, entering his apartment, engineering meetings with him, making the decision to leave Linz in the hope of being reunited with Stefan, her waiting outside his apartment, her return to him near the end of the film having left her husband, and even the act of sending the letter which gives the film its title. These are all actions which together define what can be called an action-image (or series of action-images) for this film.

Flashbacks

Again, however, this raises the question of the perception-image in this film. If the actions listed earlier are what are acted and achieved by this film, then how can its perception-images be characterized? How does this film perceive? It does so, first of all, by way of the letter. We presume that the majority of the film shows us images and sounds of scenes and events that are in Lisa's letter to Stefan. At the same time, however, many of the film's scenes are accompanied by a voiceover narration from (the now dead) Lisa. Therefore, we are being shown Lisa's memories. They are the way that she, and she alone, remembers these events. Or should we, in fact, attribute the images to Stefan's mind—that is, that by way of Lisa's letter, Stefan brings into his mind images of what is referred to? I am rather less convinced by this latter possibility, for there are a great number of scenes in *Letter* at which Stefan is not present. And yet, admittedly, these scenes might be presented as Stefan "imagines them to have been."

Commentators have bickered over these aspects of *Letter*.[47] From a Deleuzian perspective, the flashbacks can be seen as both subjective and objective. Primarily they seem to be from Lisa's perspective: they are subjective. In order to comprehend the film, however, viewers are supposed to accept that Stefan is also in some way "seeing" or remembering these images. This therefore means that the images we see and the sounds we hear are also in some way objective. They are images that try to depict, more or less accurately, what really happened during Lisa's life. There are, for example, no contradictory images. There are no occasions when Stefan, while reading the letter, suddenly exclaims, "No! It didn't happen like that!" In the end, all of this must be tempered by the fact that this is Lisa's story, so the film's perception-images are in many ways alibis for her actions, experiences, and memories.

We might be able to ask another question here. What motivates these images? *Letter from an Unknown Woman* is ordered by way of flashbacks in ways that are fairly similar to *La signora di tutti*. As discussed earlier, the flashbacks of *La signora* presents us with a range of episodes that show us, ultimately, why Gaby Doriot committed suicide. Thus, the flashbacks of the film can, in the end, be clearly placed on a timeline such that *this happened* (Gaby was expelled from school), then *this happened* (Gaby meets Roberto at a party he holds), then *this happened* (Gaby goes to stay with Roberto's mother, Alma), and so on, until we have a clear timeline that leads to the film's result: Gaby commits suicide. Does the same kind of result occur for *Letter from an Unknown Woman*? Yes, it most certainly does. We have a series of flashbacks arranged in chronological order that leads us to the film's result: that Lisa has died and that Stefan will almost certainly die too. Crucially, we also know that this has been worthwhile. It has been Lisa's achievement. Another way to see this is to declare that, at the end of the film, everything is in its place. The film has revealed to us a "true" version of the past. We can even go so far as to say that it is true because Stefan, at the very end of the film, comes to remember it as true. All of this, Lisa's life and love for him, has had no true existence until, finally, Stefan himself has remembered.

The Impulse-Image

There is yet another way to approach the images of *Letter from an Unknown Woman* from a Deleuzian perspective. This is by way of what Deleuze calls the impulse-image. Films of the movement-image—of which *Letter* is an example—will necessarily contain elements of the perception-image and action-image, with affection-images derived from these (as we shall see later). Deleuze develops some other subcategories that do not apply to all movement-image films, but which exist alongside the major image categories of perception, action, and affection. These are the impulse-image, reflection-image, and relation-image. Deleuze states that the impulse-image "is stuck between the affection-image and the action-image" (*C1*, 134), and there are specific ways in which this impulse-image comes into being.

First of all, Deleuze states that at the beginning of any impulse-image is an originary world. This sounds a bit strange, but what Deleuze means is that in films of the movement-image, there is a background of potential things that might happen. There are stimulants or motivations that will drive a film, along with its stories and characters, toward the actions those characters will perform. If we think about the action-image in terms of getting from *where I am now* to *where I want to be*, then we can also figure that the "impulse" is what, in the first place, gives a character the idea or motivation to get to where they want to be. Perhaps call this a desire or wish to get to one's destination or result. Deleuze calls this an impulse; hence the notion of an impulse-image. *Letter from an Unknown Woman* provides an excellent example of an impulse-image because its actions are not as clear and definitive as would typically be expected from a film whose dominant mode is that of the action-image. *Letter*'s dominant mode is not that of the action-image per se, but rather is of the impulse-image. Clear examples of the action-image are provided by (a) crime films and detective films—for these are based on the capturing of the criminal—or by (b) westerns—for these typically are resolved when the good cowboy triumphs over the evil cowboy—or by (c) romances—which result in the getting together of the romantic couple. These are all genres whose results, for the most part, are clearly defined.[48] Melodramas, such as *Letter*, do something rather different from these genres insofar as the outcomes of melodramas are not usually so clearly defined. With *Letter* we cannot even be certain whether the resolution is a tragedy or a triumph. Hence, *Letter from an Unknown Woman* makes the impulse-image dominant. One way to conceive of this is to claim, as Deleuze does, that the impulse-image is more subtle than the action-image: it shows us small gestures rather than gunfights or brawls.

Deleuze states that the impulse-image emerges out of an "originary world." He refers to this originary world as a kind of "background" or "unformed matter." What he means is that the originary world is the unformed substance out of which the contents—the events and actions—of a film will emerge. In other words, what Deleuze calls an originary world is akin to the wet clay out of which a pot will eventually be formed, or the blank canvas and paints out of which a painting will take shape. And what makes a pot or painting emerge? Well, such a thing will emerge via an impulse—that is, via the impulse toward making a certain type of pot or painting. For a film and its narrative, therefore, Deleuze describes the impulse-image as a kind of "how things get going," what moves things in a particular direction, what sets things on a particular course.

In *Letter from an Unknown Woman* the impulse is unerringly clear. Everything changes and is set in motion on the day Stefan arrives, with all his belongings, to move into the apartment building where Lisa lives. It is here that Lisa's life direction finds its purpose and impetus, its impulse. It is how Lisa's desire to enter another world of art and culture is sparked. It will guide both her life and the film we watch.

But where is the originary world here? To some extent it can be characterized by the courtyard of the apartment block, for it is here that Lisa first sets eyes on Stefan's belongings, and later it will be here that she listens to Stefan playing his piano. Her dream of another world with Stefan takes root here— it originates here; hence we can call it an originary world. Deleuze is careful to specify that what he calls an originary world is different from what he refers to as a film's milieu. The milieu describes the geographical setting and the historical period of a film, along with aspects of social class, of the "social milieu," as it were. For *Letter*, these aspects of the milieu are very clear. We are in Vienna at the beginning of the twentieth century, and Lisa's social status is bourgeois with aspirations— for her mother, at any rate—to move up the social scale. The impulse-image and its originary world are certainly related to the milieu, but they perform a rather different function. If the milieu gives us the where and when, then the originary world and the impulse-image give us much more of a why or how things begin to move in a certain direction. The direction in which things move in *Letter from an Unknown Woman* is in the direction of Lisa's dream to enter a better world via her love for Stefan.

As we have already seen, it is the Vienna sequences, often at night, that form the atmosphere in which Lisa's dreamworld is most clearly figured and where Lisa can be presented as glowing, as though on her way to another world. *Letter*'s characteristic of circling back to Stefan's apartment and its surrounds marks out this zone as the originary world whence Lisa's dreams take flight. Deleuze thus declares that impulses are akin to notions of hunger or sexual desire, but also that such impulses can be perverse—Deleuze goes so far as to call them "symptoms." We certainly have a perverse case of impulses in *Letter* by way of Lisa's masochism, her capacity for suffering and waiting, all with the aim of "putting on wings" and entering an ideal reality, albeit a reality that is suspended in fantasy (as Deleuze claims in *Coldness and Cruelty*).

Deleuze goes on to make complex claims for the impulse-image in relation to time. He claims, for example, that "The originary world is a beginning of the world, but also an end of the world" (*C1*, 126). And thus we can claim that Lisa's dreams are born and sustained in the environs of Stefan's apartment. But they also come to an end here, by way of Stefan's final remembrance of Lisa—only when it is too late—and thus also by way of the letter itself which he reads in his apartment.

Deleuze expands on these aspects of temporality in relation to the impulse-image. "Whether it is a time of entropy," he writes, "or the time of eternal return, in both cases time finds it source in the originary world, which confers upon it a role of a destiny which cannot be expiated" (*C1*, 127). And what better way to describe Lisa's desire for Stefan than as "a destiny which cannot be expiated," for Lisa follows this desire to what seems to be its only possible conclusion: death. Deleuze goes so far as to claim that films of the impulse-image have properties that bring them remarkably close to films of the time-image. Again, in relation to *Letter*, especially in view of its elaborate flashback structure, we have a film that seems to contain many attributes of a time-image. But Deleuze claims that films of the impulse-image can, ultimately, only present time in a negative manner, that is, as "attrition, wastage, destruction, loss" (*C1*, 127).

Alongside the emergence of symptoms that pertain to the impulse-image, there also emerge objects toward which impulses are directed. These objects are ones that Deleuze calls fetishes, clearly following a psychoanalytic path which chimes perfectly with the masochistic tendencies of *Letter*. Deleuze's use of the term "fetish" here is not, however, necessarily psychoanalytic. Rather, if we follow a standard dictionary definition of that term, then fetish means for Deleuze here an object that has spiritual or magical powers. The fetishes in *Letter* are delivered in a fairly straightforward way: via Stefan's piano playing and also by way of his hands which strike the piano keys. The film devotes key moments to these fetishes. Lisa is entranced by the world of art and culture Stefan represents, and it is by way of his piano playing that aspects of Lisa's entrancement are signified in their most intense ways.

This aspect of *Letter from an Unknown Woman* is first introduced on the day when Stefan's belongings are being moved into the apartment complex and there is a bit of a kerfuffle as the removalists struggle to hoist the piano up the complex's interior staircase. Lisa is energized by the excitement of this drama. Immediately following this scene there is a dissolve to the image of Stefan's hands playing the piano that has been installed in his apartment. We do not see his head or face in this shot. We see only his hands as they play. These are images that Lisa herself could not have seen, for she is most certainly not present in Stefan's room here. Lisa declares as much in her voiceover, saying that "I didn't see you that day, or for many days thereafter." As she is saying this, the image fades to a view of the apartment complex's courtyard—this film's "originary world"—where Lisa's words continue, "but I could listen to you playing." Panning, the camera slowly traverses the courtyard until it captures Lisa in its sights as she swings idly on the swing set up in the courtyard. She listens to Stefan's playing. This music is quite clearly what draws Lisa to Stefan in these early scenes of the film. His piano playing is nothing less than a fetish. From images of Lisa swinging we cut back to images of Stefan playing, with these views again being ones at which Lisa was not present. We do see his head and face in these shots, images that signify Stefan's concentration and devotion to playing the piano well. For Lisa, these are not scenes she is seeing, they are scenes she is hearing, and it is by way of hearing Stefan's piano that her attraction to him is sealed. In the manner of a fetish, it is as though his playing has a magical effect upon her.

A little further into the film the camera shows us a typical evening in which Lisa, lying alone in her bedroom, can hear

Stefan's playing. Her voiceover states, "What I really lived for were those evenings when you were alone, and I pretended you were playing just for me." She continues, "And though you didn't know it, you were giving me some of the happiest hours of my life." We then see Lisa sneak out of her bedroom, past her mother who fails to notice her, and out onto the landing where she lifts the transom above Stefan's apartment door so as to better hear his piano. Shortly after this we also see Lisa sneak into Stefan's apartment one day so as to admire his piano—a fetish object if ever there was one.

To continue: after Lisa has returned from Linz she meets Stefan again, and they spend a night together. The last activity of their evening is to go to a café where they dance, until the band packs up (a band of female musicians, it must be said), and, seeing the upright piano now free, Stefan ambles over to it to play. Here Ophuls delivered some of the most famous shots of the film, wherein Lisa listens in awe and wonder at Stefan's playing. Then finally, near the end of the film, Lisa tries one last time to be remembered by Stefan. She sees that he has given up his piano aspirations to such a degree that the piano in his apartment is locked and only his butler has the key. It is as though, here, finally, the piano has sealed their fate. Thus, over the course of *Letter from an Unknown Woman*, the piano functions as a fetish, as a key object toward which the impulses of the impulse-image are directed.

The Affection-Image in *Letter from an Unknown Woman*

I have tried to account, to some extent, for the perception-image and the action-image in *Letter from an Unknown Woman*, while also pointing out that the dominant image regime of the film is that of the impulse-image. How then, finally, might one account for the status of the affection-image in this film? As I have noted a number of times, perception and the perception-image arise "as a function of our needs," with the perception-image being related to the needs of any particular film. Thus, perception is related to action, and so too does the perception-image function in relation to the action-image. I have spent a good deal of time detailing how the relationship between perception and action functions in *Letter from an Unknown Woman*, with some comments also on Deleuze's notion of the impulse-image and its importance for conceiving of the film. We know by now that affection is what occurs between a perception and an action. We have also seen earlier that the impulse-image occurs between affection and action, or between the affection-image and the action-image. Where, then, in all of this, can the affection-image be located?

As described earlier, there are three key aspects of the affection-image:

1   affection is the consequence of a delay between perception and action;

2   affection involves the intersection between one body (or object) and another body (or object);

3   affections are typically registered, in cinema, on the (human) face.

Letter from an Unknown Woman, like most melodramas, offers exceptional examples of delay between perception and action, for much of the film is concerned with waiting; that is, with Lisa's waiting and wondering when or if she will see Stefan again. Many of the film's early sequences foreground operations of anticipation in ways that we have already seen. For instance, the young Lisa's admiration for Stefan from afar, by way of listening to his piano, offers examples of the delay between a perception—her listening to his playing—and an action—actually meeting and spending time with him. Thus, in the early scenes where Lisa spends time in the courtyard of the apartment complex listening to Stefan's playing, she has not even met him yet, for that meeting occurs only at the moment when she holds open the door to the apartment building one day as he exits the building. Their meeting is the action, a final consequence of the delay of affection that has permeated her relationship to Stefan up to that point. In this sense, the whole opening of *Letter* is awash with affection. These cycles of affection pervade the entire film, for *Letter* is composed of extended periods in which Lisa is separated from Stefan, and brief periods which they share. One commentator goes so far as to argue that the initial scenes in which Stefan's hands play the piano—scenes at which Lisa could have in no way been present—are only completed midway through the film when Lisa and Stefan visit a café late at night where he plays the piano, for it is only here that she sees him play the piano, thus "completing" the scene that first appeared earlier in the film.[49] This is one example of the way the film handles the separations and connections between this pair with great deftness. We shall see more examples below.

The second attribute of the affection-image, whereby one body intersects another—a "conjunction" between two bodies—is, on the one hand, rather simple to understand, for it is what occurs when one body touches another, and we are certainly accustomed to understanding that intimate contact between one human being and another may be called "affection." But things become slightly more complicated when we conceive of this in terms of cinematic images, as an affection-image, for seeing and images are typically quite distinct from notions of touching. In other words, we typically conceive of seeing as something that is done from a distance, whereas touching is associated with closeness, proximity. And yet, at the same time, we are all quite familiar with the notion of being moved by something we see, of being affected by something we witness. We may even be familiar with the notion of "love at first sight," that is, a sense in which seeing something can cause a great affective charge in us. It is notions like this—some will call it "haptic vision" (where haptic = based on the sense of touch)—that Deleuze is keen to formulate by way of the notion of the affection-image.[50]

Deleuze outlines these notions in ways that are not entirely straightforward. For example, he coins the term "dividual"—that is, a sense in which the individual splits into two parts and thus become *di*vidual—to try to explain how this notion of conjunction works in relation to affection.

> The expressed—that is, the affect—is complex because it is made up of all sorts of singularities that it sometimes connects and into which it sometimes divides. This is why it constantly varies and changes qualitatively according to the connections that it carries out or the divisions it undergoes. This is the Dividual. (*C1*, 105)[51]

One way to try to understand what Deleuze is getting at here is by way of Bergson's example of being pricked by a pin. If I am pricked by a pin, then, at this moment, the pin becomes part of me, it is conjoined with me, it makes contact with what is "inside" me. And this conjoining is what Deleuze means by "dividual"—the pin is not me, and yet, at this moment, it is (in) me, or is part of me. It is connected to me and yet at the same time disconnected from me. And isn't this precisely what happens when Lisa is listening to Stefan's piano? The scenes of Lisa swinging on a swing and listening to the sounds of Stefan's piano are intercut, as has already been mentioned, with shots of his hands playing the piano, as well as, a little later, a front-on shot of him as he plays. The intercut shots of Stefan in some way answer the questions of what is Lisa thinking? or what is Lisa imagining? (on this point, see *C1*, 88). It is in this way that the intercutting establishes a connection between what Lisa is thinking or imagining and a budding love—call it "affection"—for Stefan. The crosscutting establishes none other than the conjoining of Stefan with Lisa, and we can call this connection "dividual." We perhaps have nothing less here than the famous Kuleshov effect—or Kuleshov *a*ffect; that is, the way in which a connection between shots establishes an affect.

We in fact see this pattern repeated many times in *Letter from an Unknown Woman*. These patterns always occur in the context of the third attribute of the affection-image: the human face. Deleuze states that "*The affection-image is the close-up, and the close-up is the face*" (*C1*, 87; emphasis in original). He also claims that "There is no close-up of the face," for "The close-up is the face" (*C1*, 99). What does Deleuze mean here by connecting the affection-image, the close-up, and the face? First of all, he tries to isolate what is specific about the technique of the close-up, a technique which is, after all, very specific to the cinema. What is most specific about the close-up is that it abstracts from all spatiotemporal coordinates. A close-up of an object removes that object from space and time. (Deleuze gets these ideas from two early theorists of the cinema, Béla Balázs and Jean Epstein.)[52] This is why Deleuze refers to the face as an entity, for it is a thing that inheres in itself: it is ripped away from its relationship to other things in the world.

And yet, the issue of the close-up and the face is not quite that simple. Deleuze relies, to some extent, on the system of semiotics developed by American philosopher C. S. Peirce (1839–1914), as he does to some extent across the *Cinema* books. Peirce, as part of his theory of signs and signification, distinguishes between what he calls firstness and secondness (he also invents a category of thirdness). Objects or things which signify by way of secondness do so by virtue of their difference from something else. Thus, I come to know what up is because of its difference from down, or big from small, hot from cold, and so on. Such things are defined by way of their "secondness" because two things (or a relation between two things) are needed in order to understand them. Firstness, by contrast, designates a thing that can signify on its own terms: it does not need a contrast with something else in order to signify. Deleuze expands on this notion of firstness by linking it closely with affection. He claims that firstness is something felt rather than conceived, and that, rather than being something that is mediated or intellectualized, "it is an immediate and instantaneous consciousness" (*C1*, 98). The links with Bergson's conception of affection should be clear here. The feeling (pain) of being pricked by a pin, for example, will always precede my apprehension that I have been pricked by a pin: the feeling comes first; the apprehension comes second (and thus with firstness and secondness according to Peirce).

The close-up, especially when it is of a human face, can deliver this sense of "instantaneous consciousness." Deleuze even uses the English word "wonder" to try to describe what is at stake in such instances. And what better way to describe Lisa's face as she listens to Stefan's piano early in the film: it is a face of wonder, an "instantaneous consciousness" that is moved to the point of wonder at what is being heard. For *Letter from an Unknown Woman*, these are key instances of the affection-image. It is as though Lisa's enraptured face is transported to a zone beyond space and time to the point where nothing else matters. As she herself says, "you were giving me some of the happiest hours of my life."

Abstraction from space and time, as well as "firstness," only gives part of the story, however. I have already claimed that the notion of conjunction or connection is crucial for the affection-image. If this is the case, then conceiving of the close-up and the face as a formation that is disconnected from space and time, as well as from relations to other objects, might open up a contradiction. How can the affection-image be both an image of connection and of disconnection? We shall have to see how Deleuze makes his case.

At one point in *Cinema 1* Deleuze asks what is at stake when we see someone on screen—a close-up, a face—who is angry? He answers that we see the object—the person, the face—who is angry, but we also sense something else that is anger as such. This anger is the affect, and it is not necessarily attached to the object (the face) that expresses this anger. In a sense, Deleuze is trying to say that anger as an affect is disconnected from the object which is an angry face. The anger (the *expressed*) and the face (the *expression*) are different. And yet, it is still the face that expresses this anger. This leads Deleuze to therefore claim that "the affect does not exist independently of that which expresses it, although it is completely distinct from it" (*C1*,

97). Thus, the affect—anger—cannot exist without the angry face that expresses it, but the anger as affect is nevertheless "completely distinct from" the angry face. In short, the affect is both connected to and disconnected from the object which expresses it. It is "dividual."

Deleuze pushes even further in this direction, a direction which could be called mystical, to try to fathom just what is specific to the affection-image and the close-up of the face. He writes that the face certainly emerges as an object that acts, for it can be specified, pointed to, and described. But he wants to imply that there is a *something else* at play here. He writes that this something else is "not exactly suprahistorical or eternal," but that it hints at these sorts of things. It is a something else that seems to be beyond or even inside the face. It is a matter of an internal expression that is felt, rather than external expression that is interpreted or understood. As Deleuze had put it earlier, this internal expression is a matter of trying to characterize the way in which a subject feels itself "from the inside" (*C1*, 65).

Some examples can make these musings of Deleuze's rather less mystical. For example, if we have Lisa's external expression, that is, the expression of wonder as she listens to Stefan's piano, then what might the affect be? What is the expressed, as distinct from the expression, that is at stake here? It is none other than the depth of feeling Lisa has for Stefan— call it love, admiration, or infatuation. In other words, the exterior visage may bring one set of signs with it—a smile, wide eyes, a dazzled or dazed expression—but this will indicate a something else that is beyond that which can be precisely specified—wonder, love, something that cannot be pointed to and named, but which lies beyond the realm of objectivity. The affection-image is such a thing.

There are four key instances where the play of the affection-image is heightened in *Letter from an Unknown Woman*. I have already mentioned the scenes near the beginning of the film in which Lisa first encounters Stefan via listening to his playing of the piano. These scenes show us the young Lisa's face, swinging in the courtyard of the apartment complex, intercut with images of Stefan playing the piano, and give us perfect examples of the "dividual" nature of the face and the close-up. This kind of formation is then repeated as Lisa again listens to Stefan playing the piano when they visit a café late at night. Here, he plays the piano after the band has packed up and left for the night. These shots are some of the most famous of the film, where Lisa kneels at the side of the piano, gazing up with an expression that can be none other than that of wonder, an expression of awe. It is worth paying some attention to the way Ophuls shapes this scene. At first, Lisa stands at quite some distance from Stefan, perhaps ten or twelve feet away. But as he plays, she draws closer to him, and the camera also tracks toward them—a trademark Ophulsian camera movement—as though it is trying to accentuate their closeness. Stefan tells her, "Promise me you won't vanish." She replies, "I won't be the one who vanishes." And still the camera moves closer. By this point Lisa is kneeling down at the far end of the piano varying her gaze between Stefan's hands, and then occasionally looking up at his face. Then the camera cuts to a close-up of Lisa as she looks up at Stefan's face. Now, we see only her face. It is a face that radiates joy and wonder. She is utterly entranced by Stefan, and her face is "lit from within" (as we have seen Perkins describe it).[53] We then cut back to a medium shot that contains both Lisa and Stefan. This gives us a characteristic three-shot formation—medium shot, then close-up, then back to medium shot—in which the close-up appears as an emphasis or climax. It gains its intensity by virtue of the fact that it is a close-up. It gains added emphasis by way of its contrast with the surrounding shots, as though it is in dialogue with the surrounding shots. Once again, this is why Deleuze refers to such close-up formations in terms of their "dividual" nature.

A third key close-up occurs when Lisa attends the opera in Vienna, where she sees Stefan for the first time in many years. During the performance, Lisa is located in a box that appears to be above the height of the stage, while Stefan seems to be seated lower down in the theater. Thus, Stefan's gaze is typically directed upward as he searches in the audience for Lisa, while Lisa directs her gaze downward in search of him. Lisa, as ever, seems to be lit from within, her face radiating light and surrounded by darkness (Deleuze would call it a "reflective" face).[54] The camera tracks slowly toward Lisa as the voiceover narration delivers her thoughts to us. "Suddenly, in that one moment, everything was in danger." As she speaks and the camera moves ever closer, we cut to an extreme close-up of Stefan, his head canted slightly to one side, with the very slightest glint of a tear in his eye. This is exactly what Deleuze means by declaring that the close-up of the face removes it from all spatiotemporal coordinates, for we cannot locate Stefan spatially here. He is clearly quite some distance from Lisa, but the closeness of the close-up suggests proximity. And such proximity is at stake in the close-up. It is as though we are so close to this face, or that Lisa is so close to this face, that they are indeed touching, they are connecting, intersecting— and this is precisely what produces an "affection-image." The close-up of Stefan is so removed from space and time that it may even be merely something Lisa is imagining, as though in answer to her voiceover narration she is summoning up this vision of Stefan. We then cut back to an image of Lisa's face, thus repeating the same three-shot formation we had seen earlier, though this time with an emphatic close-up of Stefan, rather than of Lisa.

A fourth and final scene which emphasizes the affection-image comes near the film's end, when Lisa visits Stefan at his apartment for the last time. Stefan makes small talk, telling Lisa of how his career as a pianist has not gone well. He dismisses his failure by stating, "Since then I've found other things to do, more amusing things." As he states this he lifts the translucent veil Lisa is wearing so as to expose her face to us, in close-up, from just over Stefan's left shoulder. She once again exhibits that adoring gaze as she looks up at him as though caught in a spell, the same awe-struck gaze we saw earlier on the swing or at the café as she listened to Stefan's piano. Her face is nevertheless here in shadow, with the primary light source coming from behind her. They kiss passionately. Stefan decides on fixing them some drinks, and in doing so, Lisa turns so that the camera now captures her face in full light. She tries to tell Stefan that she has something very important to tell him, presumably that they have a son, and perhaps also that she is married but is prepared to leave her husband. But she does not get the chance to tell him this, for he moves further away in order to fix their drinks. As he fusses over this task, it dawns on Lisa that Stefan will never know her, that she will remain for him an "unknown woman." Eventually he utters those key words, "Are you getting lonely out there?" She replies, "Yes, very lonely."[55] And it is here that her visage cracks. We no longer have a face of admiration or wonder or awe, for now there is only a face of despair: crinkled, frowning, turned inward, crushed. And she leaves.

Some Conclusions on *Letter from an Unknown Woman* and the Movement-Image

Letter from an Unknown Woman gives us great insights into the complexities of the movement-image, especially via its primary characterization as an example of the impulse-image. It demonstrates that the major categories of the movement-image—the perception-image, the action-image, and the affection-image—can be grasped in ways that are both subtle and complex. *Letter*'s innovative use of flashbacks will also be of interest to us when we encounter, in the following section of this book, the time-image by way of Ophuls's *Lola Montès*.

There remains one aspect to clear up before we get to that. Some commentators on *Letter from an Unknown Woman* take the "imaginary train" sequence—the amusement park train ride in which Lisa and Stefan travel to various tourist destinations—

as somewhat emblematic of the way that Ophuls views the cinema. George M. Wilson tells us that "there is, perhaps, a quiet warning in this scene to an overly sentimental audience about the film that they are watching."[56] The argument goes something like this: if the amusement park train ride, which so resembles a trip to the cinema in this sequence, is deemed an illusion, then it also signifies to us, as the film's viewers, that cinema itself is an illusory medium. Laura Mulvey also makes this point, "[Ophuls] never lost sight of the fact that [film] is a medium of illusion, of play and fantasy, which the intellectual adherent of modernism exposes while the spinner of romantic tales for the modern masses might do well to conceal."[57] In other words, Ophuls in no way endorses the mechanisms of cinema, so that he is careful to ensure that, as an illusory mechanism, he is not peddling illusions. One lesson to take from *Letter from an Unknown Woman*, therefore, is the message that, insofar as Lisa's love for Stefan was illusory, so too is the cinema itself illusory, and viewers ought to take caution that they are not hoodwinked into seeing or believing in such illusions.

Wilson is even more emphatic. He alerts us to the power of works of art: "In its clarity, affective conviction, and unique beauties," he writes, "a work of art can touch the emotional and intellectual core of a receptive audience. But, selective of facts," he continues, "controlled by an interested intelligence, and potentially indulgent to ready emotion, it can simplify and deceive."[58] For Wilson, *Letter* is all too aware of these aspects of cinematic works of art, for "throughout the whole of *Letter* we are," he claims, "invited subtly but persistently to step back and consider the 'hidden' contrivance behind its narrative flow."[59] Nowhere in the film is this made more obvious than in the "contrivance" of the imaginary train ride, mere painted screens that pass in front of Lisa's and Stefan's eyes. From such a perspective, one lesson of the film is therefore beware the illusionism intrinsic to cinema!

I have already tried, at length, to argue that Deleuze rejects this kind of approach to cinema. I believe the same for Ophuls too. For Deleuze—as much as for Ophuls—film is not an illusion, or, if it is, then it merely provides the same kinds of illusions we encounter in reality anyway. Illusions are, therefore, not opposed to reality, but are part of reality. Such are the consequences of Deleuze's reading of Bergson on perception. It is on the basis of this fundamental position of Deleuze's— that cinema shows us "reality" and not "illusion"—that my reading of *Letter* has advanced. If Lisa's love for Stefan is illusory, then it is an illusion worth chasing—a "line of flight," as it were. It is an illusion that makes life worth living for her, and it is an illusion that has the capacity of making a world for her that will be infinitely better than the world she currently inhabits. The chasing of such illusions invariably brings great risks with it, but from a Deleuzian perspective, such risks are always worth taking. Such risks are ones that cinema, too, makes available to us.

CHAPTER 2

On *Lola Montès* and the Time-Image

Lola Montès offers a remarkable example of what Deleuze calls a time-image. In the previous section of this book, I argued that another film directed by Ophuls, *Letter from an Unknown Woman*, is a movement-image film rather than a film of the time-image. What, therefore, is the difference between these two films? What makes one of them, *Lola Montès*, a time-image, and the other, *Letter from an Unknown Woman*, a movement-image film? This is especially perplexing given that, in many ways, these films appear to be quite similar. They both feature, for example, a central female character who, by way of flashbacks, looks over the past of her life. These flashbacks feature various dalliances and love affairs with men. For Lisa in *Letter*, the encounters are with an army lieutenant in Linz who makes her an offer of marriage, and later with a man she does marry, Johann Stauffer. For Lola in *Lola Montès*, there is a marriage to a Lieutenant James, as well as affairs with Franz Liszt and a range of other men (in Warsaw, St. Petersburg, the French Riviera, and so on). And for each of these female characters there is also one love that is posited above all others, a "true" love, as it were. For Lisa, it is her love for Stefan. For Lola, it is marked by her love for Ludwig, the king of Bavaria. From this perspective, these two films seem to be remarkably similar.

Why, then, is one a movement-image and the other a time-image? The primary difference is this: in *Letter from an Unknown Woman*, in the end, the perceptions of the main character, Lisa, are linked to actions, whereas in *Lola Montès*, the perceptions of the main character are linked to memory. As argued earlier, *Letter* develops a rationale whereby action is designed for an assumed end or result. This is a way of saying that Lisa's actions in *Letter* lead to a definitive ending. They lead to Lisa's death and to the presumed death of Stefan in a duel. All of the past is, in this film, carefully assembled on a timeline which leads methodically from the past to the present, with care being taken to clearly show the way in which events that happen earlier on the timeline lead to consequences later on the timeline. For example, when Lisa rejects the marriage proposal from the lieutenant in Linz, a consequence of this is that she is banished from the respectable society of that town so that she returns to Vienna. And, of course, a consequence of her return to Vienna is that Lisa can once again pursue her love of Stefan. Thus, one event leads to another, one action leads to a consequence which then leads to another action, and so on. Classic film studies would call this a chain of "cause and effect," and *Letter from an Unknown Woman* adheres to this tenet of classical filmmaking. Such is the logic of the movement-image.

The time-image in *Lola Montès* works rather differently from the movement-image logic of *Letter*. There are two main reasons for this. First of all, we do not have a straightforward chronological arrangement of episodes from the past. This means that, first of all in *Lola Montès*, having been introduced to her at the circus, we are then presented with a flashback to Lola's affair with Franz Liszt. It is unclear exactly where on the timeline of Lola's past this episode resides. After the Liszt episode, we are then presented with a flashback to Lola's earlier years, clearly a period of the past that occurs well before her affair with Liszt. And much the same thing happens for other events in Lola's past: When was she at the French Riviera? When was she in Turkey? When did she first join the circus? And so on. We can say fairly straightforwardly that, instead of having the past clearly laid out for us on a timeline that leads from the past to the present, we are instead presented with a chronology that is somewhat "jumbled up."

That is one point. And yet, in the grand scheme of things, this point will turn out to be relatively minor. Yes, the timeline is "jumbled up" somewhat, but if we were to take some care, we probably would not have too much difficulty arranging the episodes in chronological order with some degree of accuracy. Indeed, this is precisely what the film's producers did when *Lola Montès* proved to be a box office disaster upon its initial release. It was felt that the nonchronological ordering of events was too confusing so that a more conventional laying out of events was necessary.

Thus, what is really crucial when it comes to designating the time-image in *Lola Montès* is a second point. In this film, it is unclear where the past ends and the present begins. The genius of Ophuls's film lies precisely here. Lola in the present reenacts episodes from her past as part of a circus show, while at the very same time, many of these episodes emerge as flashbacks. In short, the reenactment of episodes in the present become "jumbled up" with memory-flashbacks of the past. The past and the present intersect to the degree that no one can be certain where the past ends and the present begins.

I have said that in *Letter from an Unknown Woman* perception leads to action. That is, when confronted by a problem or situation, Lisa determines what action to take. Thus, when she sees Stefan again at the opera late in the film, she is determined to act upon what she sees: she sends her son away to the country and organizes things in such a way as to enable her to meet with Stefan. Thus, action responds to perception. And the film's ultimate action is the letter Lisa sends to Stefan. It is by writing the letter that the past is laid to rest and the destiny of the film achieved: Stefan finally remembers Lisa and decides to attend the duel. This might be a way of saying that, by virtue of the letter, Lisa manages to "add things up" in her mind; she manages to come to a conclusive overview of her life, of its challenges and moments of joy, and especially of the fact that she declares, in writing to Stefan, "My life can be measured in the moments I've had with you and our child." In this way, Lisa lays the past to rest. By contrast, there is no such containment for Lola. Rather, her going back into the past is part of a seemingly endless cycle. She goes back into the past again, then again, then again, hoping to find something there, hoping to find new things, new experiences, new parts of the past in ways that will enable her to discover new pasts or to invent them.

We can clearly see this distinction in the ways that these films end. The ending of *Letter* is definitive. *Lola Montès* suggests it will end in a similar way, that is, with the death of its leading character. When Lola makes her plunge from a trapeze platform, we fear that the descent will be the end of her. But such is not the case. Following a fade to black, Lola reemerges in a kind of carriage platform where she is "displayed." And we hear the ringmaster shout, "Treat yourself to a good time, gentlemen," so that for one dollar, they can step up to this carriage and kiss the hand of Lola. One implication of this is that Lola will indeed return again tomorrow to replay and revisit her past once again, to discover, rediscover, or reinvent her past. The logic of the film's ending is therefore not one of closure. Rather, for *Lola Montès* (much like *La Ronde*), the world will keep turning, and the past will continue to be remodeled and refashioned.

It is here that we can find a distinction between the movement-image and the time-image. For *Letter from an Unknown Woman*, perception leads to action, whereas in *Lola Montès*, perception leads to memory. Let us work out precisely how this distinction functions. As we have seen, Lisa is indeed active in responding to what she sees (or hears). She places herself in the courtyard so as to listen to Stefan's piano; she enters his apartment; she runs away from the train station so as to see him once again; she refuses marriage to the lieutenant in Linz; and so on, all the way up to her action of sending the letter to Stefan which frames the events of the movie. As we have also seen, there are moments when there is a delay between perception and action: the affection-image. In such instances, the potential action is diverted from its aim or result, such that the delay can be said to affect Lisa and lead to evocations of the affection-image.

Lola Montès does something considerably different from this. Instead of turning into actions or affections, its perceptions turn into memories. Thus, when Lola comes to reenact, as part of the circus show, episodes from her childhood, instead of acting out this episode—that is, instead of making it into an "action"—the film instead takes us on a journey into Lola's memories of her childhood. We are no longer in the present of the circus performance. Rather, we dive into memory, into the past. And this happens again and again in *Lola Montès*. The circus is not a catalyst for action, which is to say that any actions Lola undertakes do not lead to a result. On the contrary, Lola's circus performances are catalysts for memory, and the entire film unfolds in terms of drawing relations or connections between the past and the present.

And yet, couldn't one object that this is exactly what *Letter from an Unknown Woman* does, or what *La signora di tutti* does: each begins in the present and takes us on a journey into the past? So why would I declare that these films offer movement-images, while *Lola Montès* provides a time-image? To reiterate: the former offer chronological timelines that lead to results (even if these results amount to being the deaths of the lead characters), while *Lola Montès* delivers no definitive timeline or result. We could say that both *La signora* and *Letter* are constructed on the basis of their getting to the end, while "getting to the end" is simply not an issue for *Lola Montès*. Getting to the end is instead, for *Lola*, merely another return to the beginning (as happens too in *La Ronde*). The other point to bear in mind is that one way to conceive of how this happens is that, with the movement-image, perception goes to affection and eventually to action—and it can do so quickly (as in "action" films) or slowly (as is more often the case with melodramas like *Letter* and *La signora*). With the movement-image, perception, via affection, will eventually find its way to action. Time-image films like *Lola Montès* are rather different from this. Perception may well make its way to affection in films of the time-image—and Ophuls will often show us Lola's face so as to ask "what is this face thinking or feeling?" But rather than going from such affection-images to action, Lola turns ever deeper inward so as to find her way to memory. In many ways, the time-image offers us an intensification of the affection-image, as though the image gets stuck in affection and, as a consequence, draws us into the depths of memory.

Memory, Recollection-Image

Time-image films conceive of memory differently from films of the movement-image. To get a sense of precisely what this difference is, we first of all need to ask: What is memory? Bergson, and Deleuze after him, claims that time and memory are rather complicated conjunctions of the past and the present, and understanding how these elements are intertwined is crucial for understanding the significance of the time-image. We can first of all consider this in terms of an example I have used frequently: that of Bergson's example of being pricked by a pin (*MM*, 53). In certain cases, when I see a pin, my perception of that pin will be linked with my memories of pins I have encountered in the past. I know from such memories that pins can be sharp, and if they prick me, they will cause pain. I will therefore make some attempt to avoid being pricked by this pin. In short, my perception of this pin in the present will be linked with my memories of similar pins from the past. Seeing a pin will entail my going back into the past to some degree, so that my knowledge or recognition of the past can inform what I do in the present and the future—that is, to avoid being pricked by this pin (and by other such pins in the future). And we do this all the time with our memories: we draw upon our experiences of the past so as to inform our actions in the present and future.

In cinema, this kind of "going back into the past" is typical of the function of the flashback. Deleuze puts all this in a rather complicated way: It is in the present that we make a memory, in order to make use of it in the future when the present will be past (see C2, 52). How can we make sense of this? For our pin example: at some point I was pricked by a pin. This happened "in the present," and, at that moment, I formed a memory of the pain it caused. Now, a consequence of having formed that memory is that I will be able to make use of it in the future: I will know to avoid being pricked by pins. Therefore, now, in the present, that incident of having been pricked by a pin is "in the past," and I can draw on my memory of it and use it in the future.

This is how flashback works in films like *La signora di tutti* and *Letter from an Unknown Woman*: the lead characters of these films go back into the past in order to discover the memories they formed there. In such films we witness "the birth of memory."[1] Therefore, in *La signora*, Gaby goes back into her past, to her memories of Roberto and Leonardo, in order to make sense of them in the present. And this is even more the case in *Letter*. Lisa's flashbacks of Stefan amount to so many ways of being reconciled with the experiences of her past, as though, for example, her holding the door of the apartment complex open for Stefan is already evidence of the formulation of a memory that will determine Lisa's destiny.

Deleuze calls this mode of memory and flashback in cinema a "recollection-image." Here we can be introduced to an important new piece of terminology, for what this kind of flashback achieves is to make a *virtual* image into an *actual* image. That is, a virtual image—a memory located in the past, something not entirely material, but ephemeral, and not necessarily true or fixed or permanent—has the ability to become actual, that is to say, to become permanent, fixed, "true." Thus, Deleuze writes in a late essay, "as Bergson shows, memory is not an actual image which forms after the object has been perceived, but a virtual image coexisting with the actual perception of the object." He continues, "Memory is a virtual image contemporary with the

actual object, its double, its 'mirror image.'"[2] Memory (virtual)
thus forms at the same moment as a perception (actual), but the
task of the "recollection-image" is to transform a memory from
being virtual into something that can be considered actual. Let
us see how this works in one of the key flashbacks of *Letter
from an Unknown Woman*. I refer here to the moment when
the young Lisa holds open the door of the apartment complex
for Stefan one day, the first time they lay eyes upon each other.
What is virtual and what is actual here? In flashback, Lisa goes
back into her memories so as to find the birth of this memory,
which coincides with the birth of her love for Stefan. It is on
the basis of this moment that Lisa declares, in voiceover, that
"Quite consciously I began to prepare myself for you." And
still we have to ask here: what is virtual and what is actual? As
Deleuze wrote at one point, "Purely actual objects do not exist.
Every actual surrounds itself with a cloud of virtual images."[3]
Therefore, we must see this actual event—Lisa holding the door
open for Stefan—as surrounded by multiple virtual images.
There can and will be an infinite range of virtuals surrounding
any actual. These virtuals are things or consequences or
thoughts or fantasies that are possible resonances of the actual.
In this instance, therefore, at their most basic, we could say that
such virtuals might be "I will fall in love with Stefan," or "I will
not fall in love with Stefan." These are two virtual resonances
of the actual event of Lisa's holding the door open (and there
will be many other virtuals surrounding this actual). How is
this linked to memory? It is linked with memory because the
memory is born here: this is the moment Lisa falls in love with
Stefan. Out of the virtuals surrounding the actual here, one
comes to the fore—"I will fall in love with Stefan"—and it is
this virtual which becomes actualized. Lisa's budding love for
Stefan is now no longer virtual. It has been born as a memory
that gives rise to something which can be considered actual.
Indeed, what is created here is a clear split between the actual
and the virtual. While the consideration "I will fall in love with
Stefan" becomes actual, at the same time the possibility that "I
will not fall in love with Stefan" remains virtual (along with

myriad other virtuals that recede from actuality). This is the moment when the memory of "falling in love with Stefan" is born.

Letter from an Unknown Woman also performs this actualization of the virtual in cinematic terms. The virtual is signaled by way of the glass door Lisa opens back upon herself as though, on the one hand, to hide behind it, while on the other, also to exhibit herself to Stefan, as though in a kind of display cabinet. Thus is invoked a split between the actual and the virtual, between the "real," bodily, material Lisa, and the displayed-screened virtual self. The split between the actual and virtual is very commonly summoned up by having character reflected in a mirror—the virtual image in the mirror, and the actual image as the "real" body in front of the mirror. Lisa's splitting here dramatizes the birth of this memory, the memory that gives birth to her actual love for Stefan.

While *Letter* is dotted with instances in which memories are actualized, one by one, *La signora di tutti* achieves this transformation from virtual to actual in a rather different fashion. The actual and the virtual are held in abeyance, and in this sense, *La signora* comes close to what Deleuze calls the "Large Form of the Action-Image."[4] It is only near the end of the film that Gaby realizes that she chose the wrong route to happiness. In simple terms, her love for Roberto is revealed to have been actual, while her love for Leonardo turned out to be merely virtual. That is what Gaby's journey through her memories reveals. Perhaps, too, her acting career, successful though it has been, is revealed to be virtual, something that has delivered only a faux success insofar as it has not delivered happiness or companionship for her. Only her loneliness is actual. It is this loneliness that drives Gaby to take her life.

Image Memory and Pure Memory

Instead of being actualized, memories in films of the time-image remain virtual. This might be putting it too strongly.

If films of the movement-image provide clear distinctions between what is actual and what is virtual to the extent that a memory can be proven or considered "true," then what is peculiar about memories in films of the time-image is that they make no clear distinctions between the actual and the virtual. For the time-image, the difference between the actual and the virtual remains indiscernible (see C2, 69). Therefore, in such films, one may well discover memories, but one can never be certain if these are "true" memories. One can never be sure if they can be considered actual or if they remain virtual.

This is how memory works for Bergson, as well as for Deleuze. Memory involves a splitting between an actual present and a virtual past. It is the latter, strictly speaking, that is involved with memory. Bergson's point, however, is that the past and the present coexist. The present is always a product of the past such that the past is always part of and alongside the present that unfolds. Time splits—always—between past and present. Time, as we know and experience it, is a combination of past and present. We have no way of knowing precisely where the distinction between past and present, virtual and actual lies. One of Bergson's examples in this respect—one that Deleuze takes up (C2, 79)—refers to a theater actor playing a role. The actor, at one and the same time, speaks the parts of her role in the present, and yet, also summons up from the past her memory of these lines. Therefore, her performance in the present cannot be separated from the memory—or "memorizing"—of those lines that have been rehearsed in the past. It is in this kind of way that past and present, virtual and actual, memory and the lived experience of the present all coexist.[5]

These are central tenets of Bergson's philosophy of time. They are also key themes for Deleuze's philosophy. The latter's philosophy is nothing if not a philosophy of time. And cinema, too, offers a philosophy of time, certainly on Deleuze's account of it, so it is little wonder he was so drawn to cinema. What is so important, for Deleuze, about the past, memory, and time, and of the relationship between these aspects of what we call and experience as the "present," and, additionally, the "future"? Questions like these are central for Deleuze's philosophy.

A sense of why these questions are so important arises from Deleuze's adaptation of Bergson's ideas. Bergson argues that we typically use memories in ways that put memory to use, either in the present or in the future. We can see this in his example of a theater actor just mentioned. The actor puts her past memory of the lines to use for her acting in the present. Bergson's example immediately brings out what will become a crucial distinction. He asks, what kind of memory is used by the actor? The kind of memory the actor utilizes is one Bergson calls "habit memory." It is a kind of memory that entails use, such as the remembering of facts and figures, rote learning a poem, cramming for an exam, or learning and knowing a language (one of Bergson's examples; *MM*, 111–4). This kind of memory is linked to perception: it emerges as "a function of our needs," as I have repeatedly claimed of perception from Bergson's (and Deleuze's) perspective. And we can add that this kind of memory is linked to action: the actor "acts" her lines, and we use this kind of memory so as to be able to act on it (to recite a poem, to do well on an exam, to communicate). Some commentators imply that this sort of memory is associated with the body.[6] A good example of such a thing might be that of a baseball pitcher who will practice a pitching style over and over again in order to be able to use this particular pitch in the future—to "put it to use."

But there is at least one other kind of memory. Bergson calls it representational memory or "image memory." This kind of memory does not try to memorize certain facts or attributes of the world. Rather, this kind of memory tries to summon up a particular event or thing from the past. This is not the kind of memory that entails trying to bring something back identically, again and again, as habit memory does in the manner of a memorized poem or baseball pitch. Rather, this is the kind of memory we will be encouraged to go back into. As Bergson puts it, when we try to remember an event, "we detach ourselves from the present in order to replace ourselves, first, in the past in general, then, in a certain region of the past—a work of adjustment," he adds, "like the focusing of a camera" (*MM*, 134). But we do—most of the time, anyway—manage to bring such memories back to the present, and often we will then put such memories to use. If I am trying to remember how to get to a café I have not been to for some time, then I will perhaps dig into my memories so as to remember its location and the best way of getting there. I will go back into my memories, but only in response to an urge in the present: I want to remember how to get to the café. When I have remembered its location, I can thus put that memory to use so as to find my way to the café. In doing this, we might be doing something not too dissimilar from the way we use "habit memory." In other words, image memory can still function in a way that is rather like the way we use habit memory.

Bergson thus argues that *image memory* is not *pure memory*. There is a deeper level of memory: pure memory. This form of memory resides purely in the past such that all ties to the present (or the future) are severed. Pure memory exists out of the reach of consciousness (*MM*, 145). It consists of all the memories of the past that are in reserve, as it were, because they are not currently summoned up to the conscious present. Pure memory is rather difficult to conceive of because we are so used to bringing memory to consciousness, of making it into an image. But such acts do not give us "pure" memory. To refer directly to Bergson, "from the moment that it becomes image, the past leaves the state of pure memory and coincides with a certain part of my present. Memory actualized in an image," he continues, "differs, then, profoundly from pure memory" (*MM*, 140). Even more emphatically he claims that "To *picture* is not to *remember*" (*MM*, 135). In short, bringing a memory back into one's mind, "picturing" it, making it into an image, means that such a memory is no longer something which Bergson considers a pure memory. It instead becomes "image memory."

It is this division between a memory that comes into consciousness in the present—what I am calling image memory—and a pure memory that remains nonconscious and un-pictured that will become crucial for both Bergson's and Deleuze's distinction between the movement-image and the time-image. It is on this basis that Bergson will draw a distinction between what he calls the "man of action," on the one hand, and the "man who dreams," on the other. The former works with habit memory and image memory, whereas the latter delves into pure memory.

How can this "man of action," as Bergson calls him, be characterized? The man of action lives for the present and is committed to acting in the present. Such actions necessarily involve the body and its affections, that is, the body's interactions with the external world. Any sense of memory here is dedicated to producing actions in the external world. And Bergson goes on to argue that this man of action is therefore devoted to matters of extension in space. He acts in the spaces of the external world. Those spatial relations can be said to obey determined laws that can be measured and calculated. These laws and measurements are necessary ones. In cases like this, "the terms condition each other in a manner that is entirely determined," writes Bergson, "so that the appearance of each new term may be foreseen" (*MM*, 145). Actions performed in the present are ones that seem to obey such necessary laws. "My present is that which interests me, which lives for me, and in a word, that which summons me to action" (*MM*, 137). And, verily, we are summoned to such action, writes Bergson: "The characteristic of the man of action is the promptitude with which he summons to the help of a given situation all the memories which have reference to it" (*MM*, 153). The man of action acts, and the quicker he acts, the better.

From such a perspective, memory is geared to acting in the present (or the future). To this degree, image memory tries to function in the same way as habit memory does. We bring such image memories to mind so as to use them and act on them. We should realize by now that this kind of memory is that which is summoned up by films of the movement-image.

Pure memory is rather different from this. It does not involve bringing a memory back from the past so that it intersects with the present. It involves, by contrast, a moving away from the present and plunging into the past—diving into it and swimming around in it, as it were. To characterize this, Bergson asks what happens to the man of action when he is prevented from acting, or if he does not know what action to perform? Bergson speculates on this by asking what happens when one comes up against this sort of "barrier" where one no longer knows what action to perform so that all we can summon up are "memories that are useless or indifferent" (*MM*, 153). First of all, Bergson argues that this will result in a turning away from the external world so that one will come to focus on one's internal world. Thus, if "actual sensations," that is, those which produce actions, are extended and spatial, then they are definitely part of the external world. They "occupy," writes Bergson, "definite portions of the surface of my body" (*MM*, 139). But if we turn away from the external world we move toward pure memory. This kind of memory then becomes a matter of dealing with one's internal world. "[P]ure memory," states Bergson, "interests no part of my body" (*MM*, 139). Thus, pure memory turns one away from the body and the external world, while image memory and habit memory are matters of bodily action in the external world. This claim that pure memory "interests no part of my body" is followed by other extraordinary statements. Bergson writes that "my present . . . summons me to action," whereas, "by contrast, my past is essentially powerless" (*MM*, 137). The past and pure memory are deeply internal, they do not or cannot have effects—not directly, at any rate—on the external world. As a result, they are "essentially powerless," as Bergson claims. These are extraordinary claims, and we will see, eventually, how they function in films of the time-image.

There are other key aspects of pure memory. It is out of the reach of consciousness in ways that it is fair to call nonconscious.[7] Bergson also claims that such memories are on the threshold of consciousness. The exercise of going into pure memory seems, on the one hand, to be quite impossible, for these pure memories are aspects of the past that are not conscious. If we bring them into consciousness they cease to be "pure" memories. "[F]rom the moment that it becomes image," Bergson claims, "the past leaves the state of pure memory" (*MM*, 140). But this pure memory is, on the other hand, real. Pure memory is not an illusion or fantasy—or if it is, then such things are also real. As Bergson argues, we have no difficulty acknowledging that certain objects or parts of the external world of space exist even if we are not, at this moment, conscious of such spaces or objects in the external world. For example, I know that beyond the walls of this study where I am working there is a kitchen, a bedroom, and so on, even if I am not currently conscious of them or perceiving them. And Bergson argues likewise with respect to time: the whole of my past exists—it is there in memory, in "pure memory"—even if I am not currently conscious of it.

And yet, what can we do with pure memory, especially if we consider that it is not conscious and, furthermore, that it is "essentially powerless," as Bergson claims? Bergson tries to find an answer in the following way. "[I]f almost the whole of our past is hidden from us because it is inhibited by the necessities of present action," he writes, then "it will take [*retrouvera*] strength to cross the threshold of consciousness in all cases where we renounce the interests of effective action to replace ourselves, so to speak, in the life of dreams" (*MM*, 154; translation modified).[8] In other words, it is quite an achievement to be able to turn away from "useful memory," from memory that can lead to action, to instead embrace pure memory and enter into a "life of dreams," as Bergson states. Bergson is thus claiming that image memory can be actualized, as we do when calling upon a memory so as to utilize it for a present action. It is something quite different to enter into pure memory, for such a "going into pure memory" can only occur beyond the confines of consciousness. And yet, how do we do such a thing?

Falling into Pure Memory: *Lola Montès*

It is here that we can begin to consider in detail what unfolds in
Lola Montès. In the film, Lola enters into "the life of dreams,"
and she does so as a feat of great strength, of diving into her
past so as to see what might happen there, without any concern
for "effective action" (as Bergson puts it in the context of pure
memory). In other words, Lola is not concerned with bringing
her memories to bear upon the present so that she can use or
act upon those memories. No. The chief aim of *Lola Montès*
is to provide Lola with the chance to enter into pure memory
as though entering into a dream. Lola abandons herself to
her memories.

What, then, is this film about? A quick précis: *Lola Montès*
begins in a circus tent where the star of the show is Lola Montès
herself. Lola's act consists of restaging scenes from her life. The
film treats us to a range of scenes and flashbacks of Lola's life,
from her teenage years and her travels from India to Paris,
her marriage to Lieutenant James, her affairs with composer
Franz Liszt, another with conductor Claudio Pirotto, as well
as various other scandals in Europe. We flashback to her first
meeting with the circus ringmaster on the French Riviera, then
finally segue to her extended affair with King Ludwig of Bavaria
which the film frames as the high point of Lola's life. When the
extended flashback of Lola in Bavaria concludes, a flashback
that occupies much of the second half of the film, we return to
the circus where Lola is to attempt, as she does every night, her
daring plunge from high on a trapeze platform. It is feared that
Lola may not survive tonight's jump, for she has been suffering
from shortness of breath and fatigue throughout this evening's
show. A doctor has diagnosed that she is suffering from a weak
heart—a heart that has been broken, we infer—and advises
that she jump with a safety net in place. Lola decides that she
can make the leap without a net and does so. The screen fades
to black as Lola takes the plunge, but then fades up to Lola
alive and well, perched in a sort of display wagon, the kind

that would typically be used from transporting circus animals. Here, for one dollar, gentlemen from the audience can kiss the hand of Lola. And so ends the film.

We might believe that *Lola Montès* does little more than any standard biopic, especially one that includes a frame story—here, a circus—and a series of flashbacks. But there is something rather more complicated going on in this film. *Lola Montès* is indeed loosely based on the real life of Lola Montez, born Elizabeth Rosanna Gilbert on February 17, 1821. But one of the more fascinating things about the real Lola Montez is that she was very good at fabricating tales about her life and identity. Born in Ireland, she spent her earliest years in India, where her military father died when she was only two years old. For schooling, she returned to England, to Bath, where she received an exceptional education. When her mother then visited her, Lola fell in love with Lieutenant James, the man who had been her mother's shipboard companion during her journey from India. Lola—Eliza—was now sixteen. Her mother had tried to marry Eliza to the 64-year-old Army General who was her husband's commanding officer, a move which would have paid off handsomely for her husband's career. Before that could happen, Eliza and Lieutenant James ran off to be married. They lived for a short time in Ireland, but as James was based in India, they soon returned there. The marriage did not work out and, although they divorced, laws at the time forbade remarriage.

Eliza left India and on the journey home engaged in a scandalous affair with a certain Lieutenant Lennox. This scandal ruined her name and reputation. Therefore, soon after this, in 1842, having spent some time training in Paris, she made her stage debut as a dancer. She did so as "Lola Montez," reflecting the fact that she had embarked on a stage career as a dancer in the Spanish style. For the remainder of her career, she was not much admired as a dancer, but reports never failed to emphasize her stunning beauty and sensuality. And thus the legend of Lola Montez was born. These aspects of Lola's early life, as much as it can be verified, are covered in various ways by the film, even if some of the details are skewed—for example, a marriage in Scotland rather than Ireland; Lola on the ship back from India with her mother whereas she was, in fact, at school in Bath. But these are details treated with admirable poetic license in Ophuls's film.

The remainder of the early life of the real Lola Montez was spent on stage, more or less, first in London, then in various places on the Continent (Poland, France, Russia), until Lola settled on an extended, four-year affair with King Ludwig I of Bavaria, beginning in 1846. It is this period which serves as the high point of the film. And yet, after having to end her affair with King Ludwig, there was still much life left in Lola. She spent a considerable amount of time on the stage in the United States, embarked on a successful tour of Australia in 1855–6, before returning to the United States where she died at the age of thirty-nine, on January 17, 1861. It is worth noting that her periods in the United States were immensely successful. At one point in New York she was making $1,000 a week when $500 per year was considered a good salary.[9] In the United States, her most popular shows were dramatizations of her life, especially dramatizations of the years she spent in Bavaria. She also delivered lectures in her later years, the topics of which often offered reflections on aspects and episodes of her life. In short, the "real" Lola Montez was adept at recreating and refashioning herself. The film's circus scenes can therefore be seen as a version of these self-dramatizations of Lola's life, and although Lola never joined a circus (she was asked once and refused), it does act as a convenient framing narrative which enables the film to accentuate Lola's ability to refashion and recreate herself.

The real Lola Montez was thus an expert in creating and recreating her own past, and this trait carries over to her namesake—Lola Montès—in Ophuls's film. It makes the film a somewhat natural candidate for Deleuze's notion of the time-image. Near the beginning of this book I claimed that one of the logical consequences of the time-image was the sense that the past can change. It is precisely this aspect of going into the past so as to change it that is central for *Lola Montès* (every bit as much as it was for the real Lola Montez too). Much of the remainder of this book will look into the ways the film achieves this.

Before getting to that, however, I want to cover some aspects of the production and reception of *Lola Montès*. At the time of its release, *Lola Montès* was the most expensive European film ever produced. It had a budget of around US $2 million and could be considered a "super-production" (Müller, 26).[10] Versions of the film were made in French, German, and English. A key attraction of the film was actress Martine Carol in the leading role. Carol was famous for having starred in several bodice-ripping period dramas, especially 1954's *Madame du Barry* (directed by Christian-Jaque), so that audiences of *Lola Montès* were expecting a film that was voyeuristic and bawdy. Ophuls's film did not deliver on such expectations. The film debuted at the cinema Marignon in Paris in December 1955. The debut was a disaster. Martina Müller tells us that "Customers protested against *Lola*, arguing with the manager to get their money back." Even worse, "The police had to be called several times; fences were set up to isolate people leaving the theater from those coming in."[11] With a huge loss confronting them, the film's producers set about recutting the film, but the mold had been set: the film was a commercial failure.

If the public did not like the film, then some influential critics certainly did, with the *Cahiers du cinéma*'s critics leading the film's defense and heralding Ophuls's genius. Truffaut argued that "if the public was cool to *Lola Montès*, it is because it has been scarcely educated to see really original and poetic works."[12] In the United States, Andrew Sarris famously claimed in 1963 that "*Lola Montès* is in my unhumble opinion the greatest film of all time, and I am willing to stake my reputation, such as it is, on this one proposition above all others."[13] A restoration of the film was carried out in 1968. It is likely this was the version Deleuze was most familiar with. No doubt he was well aware of the film's history. The version of the film I have relied on is the 2008 digital restoration. This restoration is regarded by most critics as a fairly definitive one. (I have relied upon the UK release DVD by Second Sight [2008], as well as the French-released Blu-ray disc by Gaumont [2013].) Whatever the history, *Lola Montès* comes to us today as something of a European masterpiece, one of the most daring and innovative films of the 1950s.

Back into Time: The Crystal-Image

The most fundamental aspect of what Deleuze calls the time-image is the crystal-image. It is the crystal-image that can show us "a little time in the pure state." But what kind of time is it that we see? At its purest, the crystal-image shows us time insofar as time is split between the present and the past. "Time consists of this split," Deleuze writes, "and it is this, it is time, that we *see in the crystal*" (*C2*, 81). Time is therefore a combination of the present and the past. Time is both of these things: a present that passes and which, as it passes, also divides into a past. Deleuze expands on this.

> It is clearly necessary for [the present] to pass on for the new present to arrive, and it is clearly necessary for it to pass at the same time as it is present, at the moment that it is the present. Thus the image has to be present and past, still present and already past, at one and the same time. If it was not already past at the same time as present, the present would never pass on. (*C2*, 79)

At another point Deleuze will reiterate these issues, declaring that "since the past is not constituted after the present that it was but at the same time, time has to split itself in two at each moment as present and past" (*C2*, 81). To see both of these elements, the present and the past, is to see the crystal-image. As Deleuze emphasizes in *Cinema 2*, the splitting of time into present and past is also a splitting into actual and virtual. It is more than a mere splitting, however. It is also a coalescence of the two. Deleuze thus refers to the crystal-image as an image with two sides. It is both present and past, actual and virtual, at one and the same time.

What, then, is actual and what is virtual? Deleuze clarifies these points in significant ways. He writes that "The present is the actual image, and *its* contemporaneous past is the virtual image, the image in a mirror" (C2, 79). Thus, the virtual image is not, in any simple way, distant from the actual image. It is not separated from the actual in such a way as to be cut off from it. On the contrary, however distant the virtual may be, however far back in the past it may be, it is at one and the same time close to the actual, conjoined with it, connected to it. Thus, "the virtual in the pure state is defined, not in accordance with a present in relation to which it would be (relatively) past, but in accordance with the actual present *of which* it is the past, absolutely and simultaneously" (C2, 79).

The virtual past is therefore everything that surrounds the actual present, everything that might be able to be actualized in the present, but which has not yet been actualized and which may never be actualized. All of this virtual past affects the actual present in one way or another. The virtual past of pure memory is a vast repository of potential memories: the whole of the past (of *my past*, as it were).

At its most elaborate, this division between present and past, actual and virtual, is precisely what is at stake in *Lola Montès*. The present of the circus contains the past it touches and with which it is connected. This pastness conjoined with the present is played out in the reenacted scenes of the circus show, such as in the scenes where Lola reenacts her wedding, or her scandalous travels in Poland, Rome, and elsewhere. These are attempts in the present to create scenes that are conjoined with the past. Here, in scenes such as these, the past and the present are connected at one and the same time. That is to say, the actions in the present (the circus) involve scenes from the past (Lola's life). This conjunction of past and present therefore gives us one level of the actual-virtual split. And yet, this connecting of the past with the present also occurs not just in the circus scenes of the actual present. They also occur by way of the film's flashback sequences. A way to conceive of these flashbacks is to consider that they are playing "inside Lola's head" at the same time as they are being reenacted at the circus. This is to say that the past as virtual memory runs alongside the actual present and in conjunction with it as a kind of pure memory that belongs to Lola. Such pure memories are virtual, while the present reenactments of the circus are actual. The combination of virtual and actual gives us a crystal-image.

An important caveat must be introduced here. Yes, we can say that the virtual past of memory unfolds "inside Lola's head." But if we were to claim that it unfolds *only* inside Lola's head, then it would remain as a pure memory that would not have any way of connecting with the actual. We ought to remember that Bergson emphasizes the utter interiority of pure memory. Pure memory cannot be actualized or brought into consciousness. However, pure memory is part of the crystal-image as Deleuze defines it, insofar as that pure memory is brought into contact with the actual present. It is not actualized, but is instead a reverberation of the actual. "[A]n actual perception," Deleuze claims, "surrounds itself with a cloud of virtual images."[14] The crystal-image is therefore very different from the kinds of recollection-image found in movement-image films like *Letter from an Unknown Woman* and *La signora di tutti*. Where such movement-image films bring about an actualization of the virtual—memory is restored to the present while at the same being firmly placed in the past—*Lola Montès* gives us images that are virtual and actual at one and the same time.

Deleuze expresses these aspects of the crystal-image in the following ways. The crystal-image is composed of a constant shifting between present and past, actual and virtual. "[T]he crystal," writes Deleuze, "exchanges the two distinct images which constitute it, the actual image of the present which passes and the virtual image of the past which is preserved." He then adds, importantly, "we do not know which is one and which is the other" (C2, 81). In other words, in the crystal-image, the actual and the virtual shift places, they go back and forth, to the point where it is impossible to tell exactly which elements of the image are actual and which are virtual. "The crystal-image," Deleuze continues, "is, then, the point of indiscernibility of the two distinct images, the actual and the virtual, while what we see in the crystal is time itself, a bit of time in the pure state" (C2, 82). Such is the crystal-image: a two-sided image that is both past and present, actual and virtual, with no clear sense of how one side of the image may be distinguished from the other.

The Crystal-Image: Lola Meets the Ringmaster

Perhaps the finest example of a crystal-image in *Lola Montès* (indeed, in the history of cinema) occurs when the ringmaster first introduces himself to Lola in the south of France. Lola—in flashback—has just caused a scandal by bringing to light her affair with an orchestra conductor, Claudio Pirotto (Claude Pinoteau), in a spectacular fashion. Enraged to hear he is married, in the middle of a performance, she slaps him twice across the cheek before dashing to his wife so as to return a bracelet given to her by Pirotto. She claims that the gift rightfully belongs to Pirotto's wife. This furor seals her fame. (Pirotto is an invented character. No such figure existed in "real" life.) The scene seems to condense a range of incidents from the life of the real Lola Montez. Rather famously, Lola had once repeatedly hit an officer from the Prussian army across the face with her riding whip.[15] This was an act of extraordinary audacity, especially insofar as it was performed by a woman. This incident is also pertinent when—in the film; *not* in real life—Lola has her horse bolt toward King Ludwig's enclosure during a military parade, thereby gaining his attention and arousing his curiosity. Shortly after this he invites her to his castle. Together, these two scenes demonstrate

Lola's headstrong independence and her determination to get what she wants, irrespective of social decorum or convention.

The following flashback, which follows rapidly after the Pirotto incident, tells us Lola is now receiving visitors of the highest caliber and fame from her hotel on the Côte d'Azur. A first thing to note is that this scene is a flashback. As with much of *Lola Montès*, it is assumed the flashback is from Lola's perspective. The flashbacks are her attempts to weigh up her life, to discover her past, to go back into her past in order to see what she will find there. As I declared earlier, these flashbacks are reckoned to be playing "inside Lola's head," and it is on that basis that I shall proceed here.

The scene opens with the camera showing us a view from a window. The circus ringmaster, traveling in a horse-drawn carriage, comes to stop on a road outside this window. Looking out of this window, we see parts of the window frame. In ways that will come to characterize this scene, the window both reveals and obscures our view, while also dividing up what we can see. A crystal is therefore already evoked by way of the separations of the window panes. And what, after all, is a crystal? It is (so any dictionary will tell us) an object with a regular shape in which plane surfaces intersect at definite angles. Therefore, in the first instance, do we not already have a crystal, or the beginnings of one, by way of the divisions of the window pane? One way to think of this is to note that Ophuls did not have to film this scene through such panes of glass. The fact that he chooses to do so, as he so often does, imposes a certain style and shape to the images. To characterize these shapes as crystalline seems perfectly appropriate to me. It is little wonder that Deleuze can declare with such confidence that "Ophuls' images are perfect crystals" (C2, 83).

The window acts as a divider. It makes a division between us, on the one hand, that is, the place where the camera is. We see these images from behind the window. We look through the window. Therefore, we can say that these images take place in the "here and now" of the image—the actual, no less. On the other hand, the space outside and beyond the window is screened and filtered by way of that window. This world beyond the window is thus presented to us as a virtual world only accessible to us via the crystalline window panes. The camera also moves, in ways so characteristic of Ophuls, slowly from right to left. The effect of the camera movement is to ascribe subjectivity, for this may well be a subjective shot from Lola's point of view as she observes the arrival of the carriage. Its movement contrasts with the movement of the carriage we see through the window, which moves from left to right.

None of what I have said here is definitive. I have already suggested that the space inside and behind the window can be considered actual, while the world seen through the window panes where we see the carriage arrive can be considered virtual. At the same time, however, the camera movement hints at the subjectivity of the shot, thereby implying the virtual nature of a subjective point of view. If such a scenario were to pertain, then it implies that if the "look" from behind the window is subjective and virtual, then what is seen outside the window is therefore actual. In short, the actual and the virtual could here be said to oscillate, depending on what perspective we take. They are two sides of the one image, a process of continual exchange between actual and virtual. This is precisely how Deleuze characterizes the crystal-image. It is an image, the characteristics of which oscillate between actual and virtual. Here the oscillation is governed by the division of the window, so that the space inside the window may be actual or virtual, and the space outside the window may also be either actual or virtual. But they oscillate, which means that if the inside zone is deemed actual, then the outside area will be virtual, while if the inside is deemed virtual then the outside will be virtual. The two spaces cannot both be virtual at the same time, nor can they both be actual. Rather, they "oscillate." This oscillation gives rise to the crystal-image.

Still with the same shot as seen through the window, we next see the ringmaster enter a building on the opposite side of the street, the "Hotel Des Palmiers." The image then cuts to show us Lola looking out a window. The window very much resembles the one from which we have just been looking, inferring that the previous scene's point of view was indeed that of Lola. (Needless to say, the spatial arrangement here is confusing. The ringmaster enters a building on the opposite side of the street. But as we shall see in a moment, he has clearly entered the hotel in which Lola is staying, and that hotel must be on this side of the street.) Lola walks away from the window so as to receive a message from a maid (Paulette Dubost). The camera pans so as to follow Lola's movements from the left-most reaches of the room to the right, where she greets the maid. Lola is dressed in white. She smokes a cigarette. She takes the note from the maid. As she takes the note, the maid is obscured behind a patterned glass door so that her face is somewhat obscured. The film screen at which we look here is also very deliberately cut in half. A curtain slashes the space of the screen directly in half. To the right is the glass door that obscures the maid. Lola then occupies the left-hand side of the screen. We are therefore presented with another crystal-image that is invoked by the obscuring glass door and the curtain which together create a division of spaces. This division again corresponds to an actual-virtual split. Lola is here (actual); the maid is there (virtual), behind the glass.

But why is this an actual-virtual split? Where is the present and the past here? Surely everything we see here is in the present. The maid is not somehow from the past (virtual) while Lola is in the present (actual), so where is the actual-virtual split here? Or, alternatively, this whole scene is a flashback of Lola's, so might we declare that everything we see here is merely virtual? That is, it is a memory of Lola's that is both *in her head* and *in the past*? If we approach things this way, therefore, then there is still no split between actual and virtual. Rather, all is virtual. So again we are left with a conundrum: where is the actual-virtual split here? We need to be clear as to what the crystal-image achieves. We "see time" in the crystal, as Deleuze claims. But this does not mean we see a clear split between past and present, so that we can point to a part of the image and say "there is the past" and "there is the present."

Rather, the crystal-image shows us this split as it happens. It shows us this splitting before we can be sure where the present ends and the past begins. It is thus a coalescence of actual and virtual. In showing us this, we cannot be certain where one ends and the other begins. In the crystal-image, actual and virtual are indiscernible. Therefore, when we see this image cut in two, with Lola on one side and the maid on the other, we see a split between actual and virtual. The image invokes the split between past and present, actual and virtual. But this does not mean we can point to one part of the image—say, the left side of the screen where we see Lola—and say that this is actual, or to another part of the screen and say that this is virtual. Instead, the division we see shows us the split between actual and virtual, past and present, while maintaining their indiscernibility. This is precisely how such images show us time—not as split into past and present, but as a constant and ongoing splitting. That is time. Another way to think of this is to ask: Why did Ophuls not merely have Lola and the maid in a single space facing each other, clear as day? He did not do so because that would not have invoked the actual-virtual split that is so clearly signaled by way of the division of the screen and the obscuring of the maid by way of the glass doors. There is method to Ophuls's design and, according to Deleuze, that method shows us "a little time in the pure state."

Lola asks the maid to send in the visitor. We know the visitor is the ringmaster, for we have seen him many times before in the film's circus sequences. It is, of course, the first time Lola will have seen him. The maid departs while Lola walks out to the apartment's entrance vestibule. From here she can see down the staircase to where the ringmaster is ascending the stairs. The view we get is again obscured by way of a series of translucent glass panels that form a kind of glass wall that marks one end of the hotel apartment overlooking the staircase. Thus, an ongoing division between actual and virtual remains in operation in this scene.

The ringmaster makes his way to the apartment's entrance. He enters through its doors—patterned glass doors, of course.

He stops just inside the entrance and states that he is "a man of the circus." As he says this, we cut to a view of him from side-on. The shot is canted at a rather elaborate angle with our view of things titled downward toward the left of the screen. It is almost as though the camera is hiding and craning its neck in order to look at the ringmaster. Our view of him is also obscured by the leaves and branches of a plant, as though the camera is in fact hiding behind this plant. The ringmaster tells of his experience with the circus. One example he gives is finding an elephant that could play "Sur le pont d'Avignon" on the piano. As he says this, there is an abrupt cut to Lola as she listens to him. The angle at which she is filmed is also canted. While the shot of the ringmaster was angled downward toward the left, Lola is instead shot so that the angle tilts toward the right as though in a direct answer or "mirror" of the ringmaster's image. Ophuls is here playing with a back and forth of the image. He cuts up the fragments of the scene in an elaborate manner so as to invoke the crystal-image. He gives us a back and forth, a tilting to and fro, between the actual and virtual, with no clear indicator as to what is actual and what is virtual. The back and forth exchange continues as the ringmaster details many of the virtues and triumphs of his circus.

The ringmaster then proposes that Lola join his circus. The cutting back and forth between Lola and the ringmaster continues. He criticizes her dancing but praises her ability to draw an audience. The camera eventually follows Lola as she walks toward the ringmaster. They are eventually united in a single frame. We observe them from side-on, with the leaves of the plant still slightly obscuring our view. The camera then immediately tracks backward as their conversation continues. The large interior space of the apartment is now revealed to us. We see that the apartment's back rooms are obscured by the telltale doorways ensconced in patterned glass. It is as though the entire apartment is constructed out of crystal, a dazzling, glittering, but also obfuscating and fragmented crystalline structure.

Lola makes her way into one of the back rooms by way of a glass door. She is now positioned at the far left of the screen while the ringmaster remains at the far right of the screen. The plant—we can now see that it is a pot plant—sits between them. The ringmaster proposes that, as part of a circus show, Lola could reenact her life's scandals. Some viewers will know that something like this did eventually happen for the real Lola Montez, though never as part of a circus performance. Poignantly, and with understanding and tenderness—the role is supremely well played by Peter Ustinov—the ringmaster states, "We'll show everything that women dream of doing but lack the courage to do."

There is a cut to Lola, a very brief shot as she paces back and forth in the back room where she has positioned herself. The ringmaster asks her to stop pacing. What follows is a series of crosscutting shots between Lola and the ringmaster as Lola makes her way to the doorway of the back room. She leans against one of the open glass doors so that it partially obscures the right side of her face and body. The ringmaster walks toward her, and his image is reflected in a mirror as he speaks to her. The scenes here are thus full of reflecting, shiny surfaces that reveal and obscure the characters.

From here on, things become more and more elaborate. The ringmaster enters a side space that we have not seen before, a space filled with statuettes, bulbous lamps, glass screens, and other glittering trinkets. Again we can call this a display of crystalline elements. It is here that Ophuls makes the crystalline features of the mise-en-scène completely dominant. The ringmaster takes a seat in this side room. The camera occasionally glimpses him from behind a glass screen that is divided vertically into four or five panels. Eventually we find ourselves at the scene's bravura crystal-image. The ringmaster, at the rear of the shot, is framed by two large glass lamps as well as by two large, patterned glass screens on either side of him. He is screen left. Lola sits herself down directly in the middle of the screen's space. She has her back to us, at an angle. She observes herself in a large mirror which is positioned on the right edge of the screen. It is in this mirror that we see Lola's face and expressions. Our view of this mirror is partially obscured, once again, by a plant.

The reflections, duplications, divisions, and mirror images are ones that produce crystals. They abound in this scene. Ronald Bogue has done exceptionally well to describe these aspects of the crystal-image. He writes that "The simplest model of the crystal-image is that of a reflection in a mirror. When Garbo looks at herself in the mirror"—Greta Garbo is Bogue's hypothetical example—"she is the actual image, her reflection the virtual image, and the two are co-present."[16] Bogue goes on to list a number of the possible duplications at play here, such as the split between the filmed world on screen and the real world that was filmed, the distinction between the real Garbo and her screen image, as well as that between the real Garbo and the fictional character she is playing, and so on. All of these are layers of actual and virtual. Bogue then adds that these factors—actual and virtual—take on a different set of qualities under the conditions of the time-image. "[T]he distinctions between object and reflection, physical entity and its celluloid recording, actor and role, real world and fictional world become indiscernible—not muddled," adds Bogue, "but unassignable in the sense that one can no longer determine definitively the category to which a given image belongs."[17] In other words, as we have often noted of the time-image, actual and virtual, present and past, become indiscernible. Can we say that this is what happens in the scenes I have here described? Let us see how the remainder of the sequence unfolds.

The moment of truth arrives. The ringmaster offers Lola a contract to join the circus. Noting the intricate framing of this moment, it is worth reminding viewers that Lola's "virtual image" is in the mirror. She declares that she is not a circus freak. She refuses the offer. As she does so, she gets up from where she has been sitting and walks away. The camera follows her as she removes herself toward the back room of the apartment. "You know where to find me," says the ringmaster, "for better or worse." Lola replies that if she does see him, it will be for the worse. The ringmaster has also crossed the room so as to now position himself next to Lola. They converse here in a straightforward two-shot. Lola faces us, while the ringmaster more or less has his back to us. He embraces her and kisses her passionately. She tells him not to be so foolish.

She watches him as he goes back down the staircase. She sees him, as do we, through the translucent glass panels that flank the stairwell. And so the scene comes to an end.

I have so far downplayed the temporal elements of this scene. Yes, I have indicated that the scene's crystalline structures invoke the actual and virtual, but I have said little of how these elements enable us to "see time." And yet, there are temporal elements integral to the scene. The scene is, first of all, a flashback. Thus, we figure that, by way of *Lola Montès*'s overall logic, something akin to this scene will have been played in the circus performance. This flashback is therefore a virtual emanation of the actual circus performance. And yet, of course, the circus performance is itself a reenactment of scenes from the history of Lola's life, so the circus performance is therefore virtual in relation to Lola's actual history. The circus performance is therefore both actual and virtual. As for the flashback, we might say that it gives us some sense of what the "real" meeting with the ringmaster was like. To that extent, it is far less of a reenactment than is the circus performance. Thus, we could call the flashback actual in relation to the circus performance. The flashback is therefore potentially both actual and virtual. In all, for this scene, we cannot be certain of how to characterize the actual and the virtual. Actual and virtual, past and present, are indiscernible.

The flashback also unfolds for us in the knowledge of what happens to Lola in the film's future. We know she will join the circus. She knows it too—it is her flashback, after all. Therefore, the flashback brings with it a knowledge of the future; that is, of Lola's present situation as a circus performer. The flashback's images from the past are therefore intimately connected with the present and future in ways that are elementary for the crystal-image. The ringmaster's suggestions and offers, as well as his caresses—for there are indicators that, in the present of the circus, the ringmaster has become one of Lola's lovers—all enable a constant oscillation between the present and the past.

Most crucially, however, what does this scene amount to in terms of Lola's going back into memory, into "pure memory"? In what ways can Lola's flashback here be seen as some sort of journey into pure memory? As we have seen Bergson argue, pure memory is that kind of memory that is beyond the reach of consciousness. It is a form of memory that cannot be represented or imaged: it is not "image memory." Additionally, it is a mode of memory that is not actualized: it is purely virtual. Deleuze takes up the issue of pure memory in relation to cinema and the crystal-image. He distinguishes pure memory from recollection-images (see C2, 54). The latter are those that can be represented and actualized. Thus, recollection-images are of the sort that we typically find in flashbacks. We find them in *La signora di tutti* and *Letter from an Unknown Woman* where the flashbacks function as memories that come to be actualized. In being actualized these flashbacks establish the truth of the past. In establishing the past as true, the true past becomes actual. In being actualized, the true past is thus distinguished from various false pasts, virtual pasts that will not be capable—or not yet capable—of being actualized. Therefore, recollection-images, and typical flashbacks, bring into being an "image memory": an actualization of true memory that can be distinguished from various false virtual memories and virtual pasts.

Pure memory in films of the time-image works rather differently than recollection-images do. They do so because they establish no clear distinction between actual and virtual. Actual and virtual remain indiscernible. And this is precisely what happens for Lola during this sequence. She does not know what is actual or virtual here, and nor do we. I have already outlined the ways in which the circus reenactment and the flashback create an actual-virtual circuit such that we cannot discern whether it is the circus performance or the flashback that is actual or virtual. But there is something more at stake here. Lola, via this flashback, does not go back into the past in order to discover what really happened. The point of her going back into her memory is not to establish the "facts" of the past. Rather, Lola goes back into the past in order to try to think and reflect on what happened there. She goes back there not to find answers, but to ask questions. A key question—we can speculate—is that of how she came to end up in the circus when, via this memory, it is clear that she did not want to do so. As she declares to the ringmaster, if she does see him again, it will be "for the worse." To this degree, Lola goes into her memories so as to explore, to see what she will find there, and to try to determine the extent to which she might be able to find clues in her past that could be potentially actualized. And yet, we cannot say that she does find any such actualizations there. Rather, what she discovers are so many reflections, divisions, variations of opacity and transparency, a jumble of refractions—in short, a crystal-image, or series of crystalline reflections.

If that provides us with some indicators of the actual-virtual split in this scene, then what of the splitting between past and present? Where, or how, does that occur? Does the scene give us Lola in the present reflecting on her destiny? Thus, is it the present that is guiding or coloring her memories here? Or is this flashback one in which Lola manages to leave the present entirely so as to fully enter into the past as a "pure memory?" We have to say that it is neither, for the sequence instead shows us the splitting between the present and the past. If nothing else, such is the imaging function of the many divisions of the screen in this sequence—a splitting of the screen—as well as the function of the many translucent panels and mirrors. They indicate quite precisely the ways in which past and present, actual and virtual, are engaged in a constant and ongoing splitting during the scene. This is more or less as close as we can get to "pure memory" in the cinema. It gives us a "going into memory" without bringing back any definitive relations between past and present, or actual and virtual, but rather traps us—and the film's characters—in a zone whereby the distinctions between past and present, actual and virtual, are indiscernible.

Going Backstage

A little later in the film, Lola has met King Ludwig of Bavaria (Ludwig the First, not to be confused with "mad" Ludwig II). She has even by this point been a guest at his palace (a scene we shall examine briefly later). Now the King (Anton Walbrook) has come to see Lola dance on stage. It is clear that he is utterly besotted with her. It is also clear that his Queen is rather accustomed to his straying from the marital bed, for as soon as she realizes that the King has fallen for Lola, she arranges to take a holiday. Following her dance performance, Lola receives word that the King wishes to see her. Lola hurriedly tries to make herself presentable. Her dressing room is gloriously over-stuffed with costumes, dressing accoutrements, furniture and knickknacks—such is Ophuls's preference for a busy mise-en-scène. Amid this cacophony, Lola is seated, removing her make-up, while also being reflected in two mirrors. Ophuls is thus already placing emphasis on the crystalline aspects of the situation.

Lola makes her way toward the King's royal box at the same time as the King is trying to make his way to Lola's dressing room. They meet in-between, amid the props, sets and detritus that are backstage at the theater. We are thus presented, once again, with a magnificently cluttered mise-en-scène. As is typical of Ophuls, there is little editing in this scene, though the scene is broken into elements of "montage within the shot" (as Eisenstein would say). Bits of the screen are cut up by various objects: a tree here, a music stand there, a table, a candelabra, or a statue, and so on. Prominent as they converse is a large rope, hanging vertically, which we must presume is attached to the rigging above the stage. The rope dangles in front of the couple, occasionally separating them. It hangs in the foreground and thus draws our attention to the many layers of staging that recede well into the background of the shot. But the rope also draws our attention to the verticality of the image. It especially reminds us of Lola's climbing high up to the trapeze platform in the circus, for we know that, in the circus performance, she has by now positioned herself at the top of the circus tent. A pretend King Ludwig stands beside her on that trapeze platform. And thus, Lola's association with the King is performed there as the pinnacle of her life: it is while with the King that Lola's life rises to the greatest of heights. Susan White claims, for example, that this "is the high point of the film, as well as Lola's life."[18]

The rope's elaborate dangling in front of the couple also splits the screen: Lola on the left, the King on the right. It thus invokes the splitting of time that is at work here: Lola's reflections on her past while performing in the present— for we must remember that this scene is another of Lola's flashbacks—with the rope acting as a link to the actual (the circus performance in the present), while also bringing about an actual-virtual split. Here, past and present merge even as their separation is intimated. Thus, any distinction between present and past, actual and virtual, becomes indiscernible. What I mean to say is that, as we watch these flashback scenes, we are fully aware that these scenes are also, at one and the same time, virtual images that accompany the actual images of the circus—Lola's preparation for the trapeze act. And we therefore also know that Lola does not—or cannot—live happily ever after with the King. We know her destiny is to join the circus. We know her destiny is to have lost, at some point, her connection with the King.

The King reveals to Lola that he has often snuck into the back of the auditorium so as to see her rehearse. By doing so he has become very familiar with the many dance steps of her routine. He then goes on to declare his interest in Lola beyond the stage. He is interested in her ideas, he says, whether those ideas pertain to dancing, politics, or anything else. He rather expresses a preference for the possibility of their speaking about themselves, of getting to know each other, as it were.

As he utters these words, the scene cuts—the first cut of this scene—so as to focus on Lola as she listens introspectively to the King's suggestions. We can still see the rope very much in the foreground, now out of focus, with Lola positioned on the left side of the shot. As the King awaits Lola's response, there is a cut so that now the camera's focus is on the King. The composition of this shot mirrors that of the preceding shot of Lola, with a series of vertical lines punctuating this image—they seem to be various trees and other props—with the King positioned at the right of screen. After one more cut back to Lola when she replies—she merely declares that the King must be lonely—and the scene then comes to an end in another two-shot as Lola and the King gaze admiringly at each other. There are now no fewer than three ropes dangling in the foreground of the shot thus dividing the screen into an even greater number of segments.

Can we call any of this a crystal-image, and if yes, how can such images be characterized? We can certainly point to the scene's crystalline elements, the divisions of spaces that produce various splits between actual and virtual, while also ensuring the indiscernibility of these elements. And yet, these assertions are rather too vague for my liking. We need to approach this scene from a slightly different angle by asking: What is the point of this scene? In simple terms, the scene seals the King's admiration for Lola, showing us that the King means to keep Lola in Munich so that he can get to know her. We know that this is the high point of Lola's life—certainly, the film positions it as such. Ultimately, then, the scene shows us the King's attempts to keep Lola in Munich, an attempt that will later be consolidated when he insists that Lola's portrait be painted (as we shall see later).

The question remains: where is the crystal-image here? As we have already determined, the crystal-image presents an oscillation between actual and virtual, a coexistence of the present and the past, a splitting of present and past. *Lola Montès* as a whole might be considered a single large crystal which features a continual to-ing and fro-ing between the present (the circus) and the past (the flashbacks). The film thus presents us with Lola repeatedly "going back into the past." At its heart, this can be considered a matter of Lola's search for herself, for her "identity," or "self." As has been discussed at several points in this book, a good deal of Deleuze's writing is inspired by Nietzsche's dictum to "become who you are." We saw this dictum at play in our analysis of *Letter from an Unknown Woman*. In that film, it is Lisa who follows the quest to "become who she is" by performing actions that will achieve this: by refusing marriage to the lieutenant in Linz, by arranging to meet with Stefan at various points, by deciding to leave her husband, and so on. Lisa's actions enable her to "become who she is." We also know that *Letter* is a movement-image film. Time-image films, by contrast, do something rather different from this. Instead of turning to action, time-image films turn to memory. Therefore, in *Lola Montès*, Lola's quest to "become who she is" is a matter of her engagement with memory. None of this should come as a surprise to the reader, for we know that where, in movement-image films, perception is transformed into action, for time-image films, perception is transformed into memory. And we also know from Bergson that, while a "man of action" acts in the present by way of being summoned to action, the "man who dreams" instead goes back into the past, back into memory. The state of going back into the past is both "essentially powerless," according to Bergson, while also deeply internal—"pure memory interests no part of my body," states Bergson (*MM*, 139).

All of this will sound like rather too much to take on at this point, so we need something like a higher-level view of things. We need to ask: what is the significance of all this? In straightforward terms, we must declare that, in *Lola Montès*, the crystal-image is a matter of taking a journey into Lola's memories. Additionally, it is a matter of Lola's journey into her memories. She searches inside herself. The crystal-image is, ultimately, an expression of Lola's quest to "become who she is."

Much of this becomes evident by way of some perplexing claims Deleuze makes in *Cinema 2*. He writes these lines immediately before engaging with Ophuls's films, including *Lola Montès*. He writes,

> Subjectivity is never ours, it is time, that is, the soul or the spirit, the virtual. The actual is always objective, but the virtual is subjective: it was initially the affect, that which we experience in time; then time itself, pure virtuality which divides itself in two as affector and affected, "the affection of self by self" as definition of time. (C2, 82)

These sentences open up some of the most complex aspects of Deleuze's philosophy and his conceptions of cinema. Let us attempt to make sense of his claims one at a time.

"The actual is always objective, but the virtual is subjective"

In his major philosophical work, *Difference and Repetition*, published in 1968, Deleuze detailed the distinction between the actual and the virtual. A first thing to bear in mind is that the virtual is not opposed to the real. It is opposed to the actual. Both the actual and the virtual are real; one is not "more real" than the other. "The virtual," Deleuze claims, "is fully real in so far as it is virtual."[19] Deleuze will go so far as to state that "the virtual must be defined as strictly part of the real object."[20] One way to conceive of this is simply to declare that when I see a "house," then all the houses I have known before will be summoned up in my understanding or apprehension of this house. The house I see before me is actual and therefore real. But it is impossible for me to separate my perception of this house, here and now, from my knowledge and memory of other houses. On this basis I may make claims like, "this is a large house," "it reminds me of a house I once saw in London," or "this house is very different from the house I live in," and so on. These claims are virtual, but they are no less real. They inform and impact upon the reality of this house which I currently see before me. These are virtual images that "surround" the actual image, but, in doing so, they are no less real than the actual house I see before me. The virtual images make the house *what it is* for me. As Deleuze puts it in a late essay, "Every actual surrounds itself with a cloud of virtual images."[21]

What, then, does Deleuze mean when he writes that the actual is objective, while the virtual is subjective? Again we can clarify this distinction with reference to the example of a "house." I can see this house, and so can my friend who is standing beside me. Indeed, it is likely that anyone standing here will be able to agree that this house exists; that it is there is front of us. In other words, it is actual: it is actually there in front of us and thus can be considered objective. But there are also "virtuals" surrounding this actual house. The virtuals that surround this actual house will be different for anyone who lays eyes upon it. My virtual memories of other houses, my understanding and sense of what a "house" is, will be different from that of my friend. She, for example, will have lived in different houses to me, and thus will have a different underlying sense of what a "house" is. Any one person's memories of and associations with "houses" will be different and, thus, the range of virtual images surrounding the actual house will be different. In short, the virtual here will always be subjective. When Deleuze argues that the actual is objective and the virtual subjective, this is what he means.

How can such a distinction be relevant for the scenes from *Lola Montès* we have been discussing? A first simple point to note is that the virtual emerges as a product of time and memory. The actual-virtual split is therefore defined by Lola's oscillation between the past and the present, between the virtual past and the actual present. The scenes we have been examining—two of Lola's flashbacks—are part of the film's overall journey into Lola's past. This searching into the past is not, for Lola, or for us, part of a quest to discover the "truth" of the past. The quest to discover the truth of the past is typically what occurs in movement-image films. By contrast, in a time-image film such as *Lola Montès*, Lola journeys into the past not to find the truth but in order to see what she will find there, to see how various virtual pasts might be brought back so as to bear upon the actual present, the present of her existence in the circus. This is not a quest to discover a true past, but rather represents a journey or series of journeys into various layers of the past, layers that can potentially grow and expand, renew themselves. It is in this way that Lola may have the chance to invent new pasts for herself.

One of the curious aspects of *Lola Montès* is that, in the flashback sequences, Lola seems almost to be a traveler there. It is as though Lola is, explicitly in the flashback sequences, a kind of time-traveler. Martine Carol has certainly been criticized for her performance in the film, but it might be that the effect of her performance, while not exemplary according to traditional standards of film acting, in fact performs a doubling that is entirely appropriate. The effect is one in which Lola inhabits the flashback scenes almost as though she is a spectator there, watching herself and weighing up her actions and thoughts. John Belton, for example, claims that Martine Carol "seems to remain detached from her character."[22] She is, at one and the same time, being Lola, while also taking up a place "beside herself," as it were, as though constantly reflecting on or pondering her status there. I think this is fairly explicit in the scene where she converses with the King backstage at the theater. Lola is passive; she does not speak much. Rather, she observes, as though she is constantly in the process of weighing up what is happening to her at the very same time as it is happening to her. Both of the scenes I have discussed here are ones in which Lola is urged to make a decision. Will she join the circus? Will she stay in Munich with the King? Therefore, these are already scenes in which processes of reflection and introspection are paramount. These processes, especially when considered alongside the crystalline aspects of Ophuls's visual constructions, give rise to a split between actual and virtual. On the one hand, there is the actual Lola, the character who is speaking and performing in the present; that is, in the present of these scenes in which she meets the ringmaster and converses with the King. Alongside this is a Lola who has come back into the past, a virtual Lola who is entering into these scenes as though judging them, weighing them up, trying to work out what conditions and motivations led to these things happening (her refusal to join the circus; her affair with the King). This is the Lola who turns "inwards." It is the virtual Lola who provides us with gestures of internalization, of "subjectivity" per se. This demonstrates the force of Deleuze's claim that the virtual is subjective.

There can be no doubt that a similar process occurs during the circus sequences. Every moment of her circus performance is pervaded by Lola's looking back, replaying her past, going back into memory, into the virtual, even as she is also acting out those pasts in her actual performance. Thus, it is not only the flashback sequences that feature an actual-virtual split, for such a split is entirely explicit in the circus scenes too.

In earlier writings *Bergsonism* and *Difference and Repetition*—both published in the 1960s—Deleuze devotes substantial energy to describing how the virtual can be actualized. Thus, he goes to great lengths to ensure the virtual is not confused with the "possible." He argues that the virtual is real, whereas the possible is precisely that which is opposed to the real.[23] The process undergone by the possible is therefore one of realization, Deleuze argues, while that undergone by the virtual is one of actualization. The final chapter of *Bergsonism* details the various ways that the virtual can be actualized.[24] In the *Cinema* books, by contrast, Deleuze is far less interested in the actualization of the virtual. Indeed, it is only under the conditions of the movement-image that the virtual becomes actualized. What is essential to films of time-image is that they produce an indiscernibility between actual and virtual. In the time-image, the virtual is not actualized. Deleuze reiterates some of these cinematic points in his late essay "The Actual and the Virtual." "The two aspects of time," he writes, "the actual image of the present which passes and the virtual image of the past which is preserved, are distinguishable during actualization although they have unassignable limits, but exchange during crystallization to the extent that they become indiscernible."[25]

Ultimately, all of this lends weight to one of Deleuze's most difficult claims about the cinema and subjectivity, and it is to this claim that we now turn.

"Subjectivity is never ours, it is time"

We have thus far seen how Bergson emphasizes the ways in which actions imply a body and its determinate relations to the external world. From this perspective a human "subject" is made up of bodily, affective relations to objects and people in the external world. These are actions of a body in space. Such actions are determinable and obey objective laws of one sort or another; that is, natural laws pertaining to gravity, energy, and so on. We have also seen the ways Bergson argues that memory has little or no relation to the body and the external world. Memory, rather, effects our internal worlds, our "inner" subjectivity. Deleuze picks up on these elements in *Cinema 2*. He notes that Bergson emphasized the connection between memory and our "internal world," or "internal life." However, Deleuze is adamant that this is not the whole story. He argues of Bergson that "increasingly he came to say something quite different: the only subjectivity is time, non-chronological time grasped in its foundation, and it is we who are internal to time, not the other way round" (*C2*, 82). Deleuze continues in this vein, going on to claim that "Time is not the interior in us, but just the opposite, the interiority in which we are, in which we move, live and change" (*C2*, 82). These points are somewhat difficult to understand. Time is *not* in us? Rather, *we are in time*? But how can that be? I have tried at various points in this book to argue that the time-image presents us with a sense of time "as it is experienced," as distinct from the measured kind of time we find with "clock time." So, if time is how we experience it, does that not therefore mean that time is "in" us, that *my* time is different from *your* time? In other words, my experience of the duration of an event will always be different from yours; my time will always be different from yours. Isn't that what time really should be: my experience of time, not a measured, universal "clock time"? If that is the case, then how can Deleuze suddenly declare that *time is not in us* after all? On the contrary, as Deleuze claims, we are *in* time; subjectivity is time. What can that possibly mean?

A first way to consider this proposition is to consider that we cannot "make" time. We cannot conjure up time in the same way that we can make an object—say, a cake or a table. And we can even make thoughts or works of art. But we cannot make time in this way. Thus, we have to consider that time is not like that. Rather, time envelops us. It provides a something—perhaps an atmosphere, a foundation, an aura— in which we can then do things: live, breathe, act, create, and so on. To that degree, we are very much passive with regard to time. We are "in" time, and it is "in" time that we can engage in acts, that we can do things, that we can be who we are, that we can become who we are.

We need to take a step further, however, to affirm Deleuze's claim that subjectivity *is* time. On such a statement, time must be a key defining trait of subjectivity, a very bold claim indeed. While certainly taking his cue from Bergson, Deleuze is also indebted to the writings of Immanuel Kant on these points, especially those sections of the "Transcendental Aesthetic" in the *Critique of Pure Reason*, first published in 1781, that constitute a revolution in philosophical conceptions of time. Kant was responding, to some degree, to notions of time proposed by Descartes as well as Isaac Newton. Both of these thinkers made a differentiation between duration, on the one hand, and time, on the other. Duration refers to those things that can be experienced, that is, the sensation that one event follows another, so that duration consists of a before, a now, and an after. Duration is therefore objective. It is something that can be pointed to and affirmed as actually existing, so that I can agree with you that we did indeed go to the movies yesterday, and that yesterday occurred before what is happening now ("today"), and so on, all the way up to affirming objective statements like "there are sixty seconds in one minute." That is duration. Time, per se, is then different from duration. Time is considered by Descartes and Newton to be infinite, a sort of underlying or encapsulating time in which all events in the universe, in history, have occurred and will occur. This is a subjective time. It is something that humans have as part of their internal world. It is therefore distinct from the duration of events that happen in the external world. But it is also the time of God, for it is considered to be infinite and a marker of humankind's immortality, of the eternity of the soul. Kant expands on these kinds of conceptions. He affirms that time— not duration, but time as such—is not real in an objective way. Rather, it is subjective, for it is that which enables the human mind to apprehend sensible objects. It also enables the human mind to perceive and comprehend the succession of events. It is not the succession of events themselves. Rather, time is that which enables us to apprehend this succession. In his *Inaugural Dissertation* (1770) Kant went so far as to declare that time is the "absolutely first *formal principle of the sensible world.*"[26]

Kant argues in the *Critique of Pure Reason* that time is not empirically known as a consequence of experience. Rather, time is prior to experience. Indeed, it is, along with space, a fundamental underlying condition of experience. He states, "It is only on the presupposition of time that we can represent to ourselves a number of things existing at the same time (simultaneity) or at different times (succession)."[27] Although space and time are in many ways equivalent insofar as, for Kant, both are *a priori* forms of intuition, there is nevertheless a more fundamental role to be played by time. Space is a determinant of "outer sense," that is, of our sense and experience of objects in the external world. Such things occur "in" space. But time is more fundamental for conceptions of subjectivity. It is the determinant of "inner sense." It is because we experience things "in" time that we are who we are and it is because of time that we are the way we are. "Time is the formal *a priori* condition of all appearances whatsoever," writes Kant. He adds that "It is the immediate condition of inner appearances (of our souls), and thereby the mediate condition of outer appearances."[28] These are principles that Deleuze takes up and affirms—in *Difference and Repetition*, in his late article on Kant,[29] as well as in the *Cinema* books. The emphasis on Kant's philosophy of time, and its relationship to Bergson's arguments, is crucial for understanding what Deleuze means by a "time-image." Deleuze will therefore write, in *Cinema 2*, that "Kant defined time as the form of interiority, in the sense that we are internal to time" (*C2*, 82).

If Kant and Bergson provide the philosophical underpinnings for Deleuze's formulation of the time-image, then French novelist Marcel Proust provides the key elements which link time and memory, especially as is evident in his extraordinary novel *À la recherche du temps perdu* (published between 1913 and 1927). The accepted English translation of Proust's title nowadays *In Search of Lost Time* might easily function as a subtitle for *Lola Montès*, for it is Lola who searches for her own "lost time." If Bergson and Kant open up the possibility of the form of time (Kant) and pure memory (Bergson), then it is Proust who demonstrates how one can go back into time so as to encounter pure memory. This means going back into the past as a virtual past, beyond consciousness, by way of what Proust calls "involuntary memory." Such involuntary memory is one that comes to you unannounced, out of the blue, without your going to seek it. Rather, it comes looking for you, as it were. It is, therefore, not a matter of bringing the past back to the present, and thus is not a matter of discovering the present that was. Rather, it is a matter of encountering the past *as it never was*. And such a thing happens very early on in Proust's novel, when the narrator tastes the tea into which had been dipped one of those cakes, he tells us, known as "petites madeleines." And it is by virtue of this taste that the narrator is transported back into memory, into the past in which, on Sunday mornings in Combray, he had been given such petites madeleines by his aunt Léonie. As Proust puts it so remarkably, "And at once the vicissitudes of life had become indifferent to me, its disasters innocuous, its brevity illusory—this new sensation having had its effect, which love has, of filling me with a precious essence; or rather this essence was not in me, it *was* me."[30]

The key element Deleuze takes from such experiences in Proust is not that the-madeleine-in-the-present simply reminds Proust's narrator of a past moment or experience. Rather, what Deleuze emphasizes is that this reminiscence erupts for the narrator in such a way that had never actually happened in the past. He experiences the past as new, as something that has never happened before in quite *this* way. "Combray rises up," writes Deleuze, "not as it was experienced in contiguity with the past sensation, but in a splendor, with a 'truth' that never had an equivalent in reality."[31] In short, Proust's narrator experiences these things as though for the first time. The past rises up not as something repeated or even actively remembered, or as "something that has happened before." It rises up as something that is experienced for the first time, in a way that had never happened before. I think this gives us a way of figuring, by way of memory, how we can be said to *in* time, for it is by way of this memory that time envelops Proust's narrator: it places him *in* time. As I will go on to argue, much the same process occurs for Lola in *Lola Montès*.

"Affect is experienced in time, while time can be defined as 'the affection of self by self'"

These claims, once again, are difficult ones made by Deleuze. Earlier I wrote that, in the context of the movement-image, affection is defined as a delay between a perception and an action as well as being the intersection between one body and another body or thing. Finally, affection is also typically expressed by way of the human face. How, then, is affection or the affection-image relevant for the time-image? First of all, we should note Deleuze's assertion that "affect is experienced in time," for this clearly must be the case. Affection is, after all, a delay between perception and affection. Time is therefore fundamental for affect and affection. A next issue to consider is that, under the conditions of the movement-image, perception is transformed into action, even if it is delayed by affection. By contrast, under the conditions of the time-image, affection is delayed indefinitely. For the time-image, perception is never transformed into action. Perception, as it were, gets stuck in affection, the delay goes on, and instead of being transformed into action, perception is transformed into memory.

A third point. If affection is defined as the intersection between one body and another body or thing, then for the time-image, this becomes an intersection between the body and its memories. Deleuze here defines time as "the affection of self by self," so this affection, for the time-image, is a matter of the self being subjected to memory, being "intersected" by memory. Deleuze clarifies many of these issues in his late essay on Kant. He emphasizes the ways that time and memory bring about a splitting of the self. He describes this as a split between the I [*je*] and the self [*moi*]. He claims that, for Kant, the I and the self are "separated by the line of time."[32] Deleuze goes on to argue that "time is the formal relation through which the mind affects itself, or the way we are internally affected by ourselves. Time can thus be defined," he adds, "as the affect of the self by itself."[33] Again, these are bold statements, that time is the way we relate ourselves to our selves, the way that we project or reflect our selves back to us. Emphasizing once again that we are *in* time, Deleuze concludes by stating that "[i]nteriority constantly hollows us out, splits us in two, doubles us, even though our unity subsists."[34]

All of this is a way of bringing us to the point where the "self" in films of the time-image effectively takes on a crystalline form. The splitting of time between the present and the past, the actual and the virtual, is itself brought out—exemplified, expressed—by the splitting of the subject between the I and the self. This is the ultimate goal of *Lola Montès*: to depict Lola herself as a crystal.

Where or how does this happen? It happens across the entire film, I would claim, but there are some key moments where it is highlighted. Quite early in the film, for example, Lola reenacts her wedding in an elaborate part of the circus act. Ophuls's preference for a cluttered mise-en-scène is again evident as all sorts of props, costumes, and glittering forms pervade the scene, all captured by a ceaselessly moving camera. Lola is dressed all in white. All she can say here is "I don't know what's wrong with me, but my life is whirling in my head." She is kneeling and rotates slowly on a dais. She wears a tiara, sparkling and magnificent. Eventually, via a long dissolve we enter the scenes of a flashback to her married life with Lieutenant James (Ivan Desny). We are shown scenes of her unhappy marriage—James is a tyrant, a drunkard, and a womanizer—before we cut back to the circus. The ringmaster proclaims wryly, "That peaceful life couldn't last forever." Such a proclamation points to the clear discrepancy between the glory of the wedding reenactment at the circus and the dark truth of Lola's married life—an actual-virtual split, in other words. The scene continues with the extraordinary spectacle of Lola riding on a mini-railway engine as part of the circus act. She enters the circus ring and gets up off the train. At this point the ringmaster tells us Lola was destined for fame and fortune while, in the act, men with 1,000-franc coins for heads throw money at her. This scene then continues as we hear that Lola longed to become a ballerina; that she became a dancer in the Spanish style; that she danced in Rome and Warsaw; and much more besides. In short, we are here taken on a whirlwind tour of aspects of Lola's past. In doing so, we see a number of different Lolas as they parade in front of the camera, again through Ophuls's luscious, busy mise-en-scène. Susan White, in her DVD commentary on this scene, claims that "Lola is performing the identities she wishes to have." These multiple Lolas are also split between the present and the past—the present of the circus reenactments, on the one hand, and, on the other, the past that these reenactments are trying to summon up, the past they are trying to go back into. Thus, each one of these Lolas is herself split between a present and a past, a series of multiple pasts. This scene, with its splittings and multiplications, is getting us very close to a Deleuzian conception of subjectivity, certainly insofar as such a conception pertains to the time-image. It is no wonder Lola will declare, "my life is whirling in my head."

But we should ask: where can we find, in this scene, a clear notion of the "affection of self by self?" Quite simply, the self is affected by the memories of the self—a "splitting in two," as Deleuze puts it in the Kant essay. The affection occurs by way of being affected by memory: that is, affected by the past. In the same way as a pin prick will give rise to affection, as we saw in Bergson's example of being pricked by a pin, then so too can a memory function in much the same way: memories can intersect us, prick us. When memories intersect us, they make us into something different—they change us. And it is this process of change that Lola is continually going through during *Lola Montès*. The process of the film is itself one in which Lola tries to fashion new selves, again and again, by opening up new perspectives on and new understandings of her past, of trying to see in those pasts what she has not been able to see before. In short, for Lola, her journeys into the past, whether by reenactment or flashback, are a matter of trying to recover the past as new, to discover the past as it never was.

The Spectacle of Woman

Much commentary on *Lola Montès* has laid emphasis on the commodification of Lola, and thus on the commodification of woman, especially the woman as a performer, the "woman as spectacle." The notion of the woman as spectacle, as "bearer of the look," as that which on screen is defined by her "to-be-looked-at-ness," is central to Laura Mulvey's pivotal 1975 essay "Visual Pleasure and Narrative Cinema."[35] It may come as no surprise, therefore, that Mulvey herself has offered a reading of Lola Montès along such lines. The key to the film, for Mulvey, is that it offers us "the commodification of the woman as spectacle."[36] In a similar vein, Susan White proposes that Lola Montès is one of Ophuls's "fallen woman" films, films about women who were great or who had potential, but who end up used and abused in one way or another.[37] She emphasizes that in such films, Ophuls never fails to point to the ways in which society, morality, "culture," and history bring about the descents of these women: it is never the fault of the women themselves—and we have seen as much in our readings of La signora di tutti and Letter from an Unknown Woman. In a recent reading of the film, John Belton offers a Brechtian-inflected analysis in which he argues that Lola is "[t]he product of male fantasy and imagination, created by and for men."[38] Belton stresses that such a view of Lola is mainly reserved for the circus sequences where she performs under the direction of the ringmaster and for the delight and pleasure of what seems to be a predominantly male audience.

Both Mulvey and Belton take such suggestions even further. Mulvey is perhaps most explicit in this respect, for she ties the notion of the spectacle of woman closely to the notion of the spectacle of cinema. She argues that, if the woman is paraded as a spectacle here, then it is a spectacle of which Ophuls is critical. And, by extension, Lola Montès is also demonstrating to us that cinema too is a spectacle, a spectacle that typically relies on the exploitation and commodification of women, especially dazzling, exhibitionist women like Lola Montès. Thus, Lola Montès also provides us with a critique of what Mulvey refers to as "the illusory nature of the film strip and its images."[39] Belton makes similar claims, though he does so by characterizing Lola as a symbol of nineteenth-century romanticism. In the end, Belton argues, Lola Montès gives us access to such romanticism "through the illusion of the movies."[40] The film shows us illusion, but, in doing so, it is also offering up a critique of its own processes of illusion-making. As Belton puts it, "It is a spectacle about spectacle."[41]

Both of these readings are somewhat overblown, I feel, and they offer up arguments that belong more rightly to an earlier age of film studies. Mulvey's essay "Visual Pleasure," for example, was first published in 1975, several years before Deleuze's *Cinema* books. And even as Mulvey refers extensively to Deleuze in her article on *Lola Montès*, there is little doubt her claims fall far short of the kinds of arguments Deleuze proposes for the film. White, in contrast to Mulvey and Belton, resists the urge to denigrate spectacle in order to argue that "It is . . . important not to succumb to the simplistic notion that spectacle is simply 'bad': certainly Ophuls did not."[42] This brings us back to the terrain of one of Deleuze's main claims about Ophuls's style. Insofar as Ophuls's films show us spectacle, they do not provide a critique of spectacle. Instead, the scenes of these films provide situations, argues Deleuze, "where the characters belong to the real and yet play a role. In short," he continues, "it is the whole of the real, life in its entirety, which has become spectacle" (*C2*, 83–4).

Perhaps the finest condensation of these issues occurs during the sequence in which King Ludwig arranges for Lola's portrait to be painted. The sequence begins with the King's attempts to find a suitable painter for the portrait. As is typical of Ophuls, the scene is elaborately staged with perhaps two dozen or more artists crammed into a well-lit room in the King's palace. It is here that they are charged with presenting their work to the King. The artists here are given the expectation that the portrait must be painted as quickly as possible, for it is unclear how long Lola will be able to remain in Munich. Therefore, each of the painters tries to emphasize his speed (they are all male). One claims to have painted his latest canvas in a mere seventeen days, only to then correct himself by declaring it was sixteen and a half days. Another claims six weeks for his canvas, another a mere seven days, until finally one declares that his canvas took him three months and ten days. The King is impressed—and he barely even looks at this man's painting! He instantly gives this painter the commission. It becomes clear—and we have known it all along—that the King was actually trying to find the painter who would take the longest to paint the portrait, for the longer it takes, the longer Lola will have to stay in Munich. Such was the King's design.

The painting of the portrait then becomes a drawn-out affair, much to the King's delight. Lola dresses in a number of set-ups and modeling poses, poses that resemble the kind which would typically be used for an advertising campaign. (It is no secret that Ophuls detested advertising.)[43] At first a snow scene is painted, but the King considers this a little too stiff and formal. He offers the painter another three months to re-do the portrait. At this point the film fades back to the circus where the ringmaster assures us that the painting went through several phases, most of which required the removal of one layer of clothing after another. Eventually the painter presents the King with a nude portrait in the manner of Ingres "Odalisque" (1814)—indeed, the painting is a direct copy of Ingres's canvas but with Lola's head replacing that used by Ingres. Needless to say, the painting is considered too scandalous to be hung in any public gallery. It then provides Ludwig with an excuse to buy Lola her own palace: she can then hang the painting there. Lola declines this offer, declaiming that it would be too much like advertising!

The sequence, if nothing else, once again demonstrates the all-pervasiveness of the crystalline regime in *Lola Montès*. The sequence presents an elaborate demonstration of a crystal-image composed of the self and its image, this time not in a mirror, but in a painted portrait. It is a portrait that is a clear and unashamed copy of Ingres's famous canvas—a "fake," we might call it; designating it a "simulacrum" would be appropriately Deleuzian.[44] The aim of the portrait is not to capture the "true" or "authentic" identity of Lola. Rather, what the sequence emphasizes is Lola's penchant for trying out different roles, of donning different costumes, of striking varied poses. Therefore, if the crystal-image opens a split between the self and its image, between a self and an I, and thus a split between the present and the past, between the actual and virtual, then that initial splitting can ultimately proliferate and multiply, as it does here. And this is what *Lola Montès* leaves us with: not with a true Lola, not with a Lola who has an essence or character trait that will definitively single her out. Rather, we are left with multiple Lolas, none of which is better or more important or more authentic than any of the other Lolas. And this too is what Lola discovers by way of her many journeys into the past: that she is not tied down to a single identity. Her identity is multiple and is composed of multiple selves, and will continue to be composed of such multiple selves the more and more she journeys into her past, night after night. As Belton puts it, "Lola is . . . condemned to review the events of her life night after night."[45]

From Passive Affections to Passive Affections

Belton is mistaken to argue that, in *Lola Montès*, a clear distinction can be made between the circus scenes and the flashbacks.[46] The circus scenes, he argues, offer spectacle while the flashbacks offer narrative, though by narrative Belton means something like an "historical real"—he refers to the Lola of the flashback scenes, for example, as the "real Lola."[47] In other words, the circus scenes offer us a "fake" version of Lola, one that is about display, money-making, and putting on a show. The flashback scenes, by contrast, show us the "real" Lola, not sullied by the fraudulence of the circus spectacle. In Deleuzian terms, we might consider that Belton here is proposing that the circus scenes are virtual, in the sense that they are fake and illusory, while the flashback scenes are actual: they are real or true. And yet, as we should know all too well by now, a properly Deleuzian approach to these images as time-images would declare the circus scenes neither actual or virtual, and so too for the flashback scenes. Rather, both foreground the indiscernibility of the actual and the virtual.

All the same, it is worth persevering with Belton's claims, especially if we place them alongside one of the most sophisticated and convincing readings of *Lola Montès*, that undertaken by Kaja Silverman in her book, *The Subject of Semiotics*, published in 1983. Silverman argues that Lola manages to transcend the passive role typically accorded women in narrative cinema. In short, Lola offers a rejoinder to Laura Mulvey's thesis that, in traditional narrative cinema, women must accept their passivity in the face of an active, male hero. Silverman argues that Lola is at some points passive, but at other points active. For Silverman, Lola is rendered passive during the circus sequences. There, she must submit to the pronouncements and directions of the ringmaster, while also making herself desirable to the largely male audience. The flashback sequences, by contrast, feature an active Lola who is in control of her destiny. She takes control of her life in many ways—by marrying Lieutenant James so as to escape the control of her mother, and then by divorcing him so as to escape his controlling efforts. She is also active in the scenes with Pirotto, and when she rides on horseback during the military parade in Bavaria so as to present herself to the King, and much more besides. In these flashback scenes where she is active, Lola also remains attractive to the men whom she encounters. She presents herself to men as a "spectacle," Silverman argues, but, in doing so, she manages to control the "male gazes" directed toward her. "Lola exercises fascination and control," writes Silverman, "over numerous males gazes through an elaborate masquerade, an on-going performance in which she both scripts and constantly changes the parts she plays."[48] In this way, Lola challenges the traditional cinematic split between passive female and active male.

Silverman's argument is a strong one. Nevertheless, she bends *Lola Montès* rather too far so as to suit that argument. *Lola Montès* may well be an overtly feminist film, but it does not achieve this by transforming passivity into activity. As something of a proof, we can quite simply state that Lola ends the film as part of the circus, in a cage, with men paying money in order to kiss her hand. This ending hardly represents the triumph of an active woman. Silverman may well counter such arguments by claiming that the film's ending remains true to the film's feminist critique, but there is another and better way to approach these issues.

What is the relationship between passivity and activity? A Deleuzian approach would emphasize and focus on the importance of what Spinoza termed "passive affections," a notion we encountered earlier in this book. The basic Spinozian question is, how do I transform passivity into activity?—or, how do I make passive affections into active affections? And Spinoza is quite clear on how this is done: a passion ceases to be a passion as soon as I comprehend and understand it clearly.[49] As Deleuze puts it in *Expressionism in Philosophy*, "A mind that forms an adequate *idea* is the adequate *cause* of the ideas that follow from it: this is the sense in which it is active."[50] The question of how one comes to comprehend or understand a passive affection is, however, not at all straightforward.

As we saw earlier, Deleuze claims that there are three steps to transforming passive affection into active affection:

1) First of all, the passive affection must be registered, and this typically happens by experiencing or feeling something that initially cannot be comprehended—a pain has emerged in my arm, for example.

2) Secondly, having experienced a passive affection, one will be inclined to ask oneself, what has caused this affection? And one will, in various ways, try to fathom what, how or why such a thing has occurred—why am I experiencing this pain in my arm? To then work toward comprehending and understanding this passive affection—the pain in my arm—I will try to fathom other occasions on which I have had such an experience of pain in my arm, and also, by way of my perceptions, I will see an object that has pierced the skin of my arm.

By way of what Spinoza calls "common notions," I will therefore make connections between what I am feeling now, the pain in my arm, memories of similar kinds of pain I have had in the past, and my perception of the object (a pin) that has pierced my skin. On the basis of these connections ("common notions") I can then move to the final point.

3) Here, I come to some sort of conclusion as to why I have this pain in my arm; that is, I come to understand that it has been caused by the pin than has pierced my skin. It is now an active affection, one which I can comprehend and understand.

We can note something akin to these processes in *Lola Montès*. Lola may feel one thing while she is performing at the circus, these are passive affections. Those passive affections then typically trigger movements back to the past by way of flashback. We can surmise that she is asking something like: how is what I am feeling now related to the way something like this event happened in the past? Thus, when Lola is raised high up to the trapeze platform in the circus, this then sends her back into her past, via flashback, where she recalls the "high point" of her life: the time she spent with King Ludwig. In short, by way of these flashbacks she travels into her memory: Lola is trying to make sense of her past. Lola might try to make sense of her past, but she never gets to the point where she does in fact make sense of it. What is significant about Lola's journey in *Lola Montès*, and it is a point that is typical of time-image films, is that she never reaches a point where the transformation from passive affections to active affections is complete. Rather, *Lola remains stuck in the realm of passive affections*. Lola never gets to the point where she has a clear and distinct idea of what has happened to her. Instead, her destiny is to endlessly, repeatedly play over those passive affections, to the point where, perhaps, finally, she will discover some entry to active affections. And yet, perhaps she will never discover those clear and distinct ideas, and that does not matter. Going back into the past, trying to change the past, endeavoring to see what the past holds up to her: that is the point of *Lola Montès*.

The prime example of Lola's going back into the past, but bringing back from that past nothing but confused ideas, emerges in the final moments of her flight from Bavaria. If nothing else, the history of the real Lola Montez during these events is extraordinary. The population of Bavaria was, for the most part, vehemently opposed to the King's association with Lola, for they believed she had led Ludwig astray and they saw her as a moral affront to the greater glory of Bavaria. The consequences of these events, events that were part of the general wave of insurrections in Europe in 1848, was that King Ludwig stepped down from the throne: his devotion to Lola Montez cost him the throne. There is no sense in which he gave up the throne reluctantly. The King rather seems to have wearied of his duties and stepped down in Bavaria's best interests. The film stages some of these incidents with great drama. The King and Lola are seen taking shelter in Lola's palace and protestors can be heard outside the walls. Fittingly, Ludwig reads from Shakespeare's *Hamlet*, Act 1, Scene 2—"How weary, stale, flat and unprofitable / Seem to me all the uses of this world!" They are interrupted by the protests and cannot continue their leisurely evening. In a touching scene, Lola urges the King to return to his Queen, for he must be seen to be defending tradition and authority. They say their farewells: it will be the last time they see each other.

Shortly thereafter, Lola rushes to her carriage and, on the way, meets the young student whom she had initially met on her way to Munich. (And that earlier scene is another marvelous one: Lola and the student make love in her carriage as they journey toward Munich.) The student is played by Oskar Werner, who will subsequently be immortalized as Jules in François Truffaut's *Jules et Jim* (1961). He praises Lola as the symbol of love and freedom, and declares that she has inspired the left-wing elements of the uprisings. Her departure has the effect, so we hear certain attendants and carriage drivers declare, of saving the royal house and Bavaria from civil war. Traveling away from Munich with this student in her carriage, Lola toys with the idea of settling down with him. They could live a simple life, get married, have some children, and so on. (Needless to say, Ophuls finds superb crystalline ways of filming these scenes inside the cramped space of a carriage. He tends to divide the image by way of a chimney stack which emerges from a stove in the middle of the carriage.) Inevitably, Lola tells the student that they cannot stay together. She claims to have loved the King very much and tells the young man, "Someday you'll learn that people keep hoping for miracles. That's when you'll find happiness." But she adds, as the scene ends, "Bavaria was my last chance at happiness. My last hope of a haven. It's all over . . . all over." And so comes to an end the final flashback of the film.

The point of all this is to declare that Lola never gets beyond passive affections. By going back into the past, she gets "stuck," as it were, in the second of the steps noted earlier. She searches so as to try to find reasons for her situation—how did things come to this? How did I end up in the circus? How can I sum up the love I felt for King Ludwig? And so on. Lola never finds definitive answers to these questions and thus never develops clear and distinct ideas about her past. Rather, her ideas of the past remain confused, and this is why she must return, again and again, to her past, night after night, as she tries to fathom her past, her memories, her life. And here we have a great distinction between the time-image and the movement-image. Films of the time-image never quite find their way to action. They get stuck in memory, as it were. Movement-image films, by contrast, find their way to action. They discover, in one way or another, "active affections."

The Three Passive Syntheses of Time

Does this therefore mean that time-image films are failures? They are films that get stuck in the past, unable to complete their actions. From a Deleuzian perspective, the completion of an action is certainly a worthwhile aim, for life would be inconceivable without such actions. However, the purpose of the time-image is to show us the kind of life that is freed from being determined by the precepts of action. As we saw in the first part of this book, the perception-action circuit is governed by a mathematical type of thinking, where "mathematical" means calculable, measureable, and determinable—that is, where quantity rather than quality is at stake (see Bergson *CE*, 26–7, 171). This focus on measurement and calculation produces the kinds of results—actions—that we see in movement-image films, where characters perform actions that produce results. The crucial question for Deleuze, however, is how can these characters really be certain that the results they achieve are worthwhile? In other words, movement-image films, in ways discussed earlier in this book, tend to close down the past: they perform actions, achieve results, and come to conclusions that can be considered definitive. What happens for characters in time-image films is that they are no longer satisfied by the results they have found, or, to put it another way, they are no longer motivated by the need for a result. Rather, they are looking for something else: a belief, a sense of significance, or achievement, perhaps; a looking back to try to fathom their place in the world. At the limit they are searching for what Deleuze calls "belief in this world" (*C2*, 181–2).[51] To get to such a point often requires a complete redrawing of the coordinates of one's world; a reconceiving of the world. And the way that this occurs in films of the time-image is not by way of actions performed in the external world. Instead, characters in such films will withdraw into their internal worlds, into time, into the past and memory.

Philosophically, Deleuze theorized this "going into time" as something available to thought and experience by way of what he called the "three syntheses of time" in *Difference and Repetition*. The theses advanced there provide the ultimate foundation for the distinction Deleuze makes between the movement-image and the time-image. First of all, we must consider what question Deleuze is trying to answer with these three syntheses. He is trying to consider how we experience things "in" time, or how we experience time as such. Of course, this also amounts to trying to account for how we experience anything at all, for time is foundational for our experiences. And Deleuze considers that there are three dimensions to that experience of time, the three passive syntheses. The three syntheses operate together in every experience we have, though one synthesis may be dominant.

The first synthesis—the "synthesis of habit"—is one that situates us in the "now" of the present. That is, our minds and bodies are set up in such a way that we are "dialed in" to what is happening now. We are conscious of this now (though not necessarily so), and it is this now that constitutes our experience of the present. Such an experience does not include memory, even though this "now" must be experienced in the context of a past and future that are excluded. When the past and the future are excluded, we are left with the present. "This is by no means a memory," claims Deleuze, "nor indeed an operation of the understanding."[52] Rather, it is the contraction of all sensations to the "now" point, the instant that is happening now, a "perpetual present."[53]

In the second synthesis, the mind discovers the past. It is by way of the second synthesis that we come to realize that the "now" I am experiencing can be distinguished from other experiences I have had in the past. No longer in a perpetual present, I realize a past that unfolds alongside—or "behind"—the present and which is different from the present. The present is now, while the past was then. Here, Deleuze argues, "the past is then no longer the immediate past of retention but the reflexive past of representation."[54] This ability to separate the present from the past is the outcome of the second synthesis of time.

The first and second passive syntheses can act in concert to produce active syntheses. They produce memory, learning, and intelligence, because one learns that the past influences the present and the future.[55] As Deleuze puts it, "Underneath the self which acts are little selves which contemplate and which render possible both . . . action and the active subject."[56] In short, it is the first two syntheses that deliver a perception-action circuit, the kind of circuit we will find in films of the movement-image.

The third synthesis is the most difficult to understand, but it is one which we have already encountered in the context of "pure memory." The third synthesis of time is the empty form of time that is the foundation of our experiences. It provides the foundation for the way that events happen "in" time. It is the time in which experiences emerge. As we saw earlier, we are very much passive with regard to time. We are "in" time, and it is "in" time that we can perceive things, do things, and become who we are. That is the function of the third synthesis. And as we also saw earlier, this pure form of time also induces a subjective splitting in us, what Deleuze here calls a "fractured self"; a division between the self and the I. Deleuze links the third synthesis with a range of points—the figures of Oedipus and Hamlet ("time is out of joint") are crucial. But he also links this synthesis with Nietzsche's conception of the "eternal return" and the additional idea of a "belief in the future."[57] Essentially what all of this boils down to is a conception of an open form of time and, therefore, an open form of the past, a past that is not closed down, but a past that remains open, susceptible to change.

All of these aspects are crucial. Events happen "in" time, but the third synthesis enables us to understand the fact that time is open, that time does not determine what happens, but rather provides a "surrounding" in which anything at all can emerge. If the second synthesis provides clear and distinct separation between the past and the present such that it places the past fairly and squarely in the past, then the third synthesis has the ability to reopen the past. The third synthesis is the most important one for considering the time-image.[58]

Peaks of Present, Sheets of Past

There remain two elements of the time-image to detail in relation to *Lola Montès*. They are, first of all, *peaks of present and sheets of past*, and, secondly, *the powers of the false*. I shall deal with the former of these in this section, then conclude my analysis of *Lola Montès* with the latter.

According to Deleuze, time is constantly splitting into present and past. Time thus always delivers both *presents which pass* and *pasts which are preserved*. Time-images can therefore either be grounded in the present, such as they are in the circus scenes in *Lola Montès*, or they can be grounded in the past, as they are in *Lola Montès*'s flashback scenes. What, then, are "peaks of present?" In *Lola Montès*, these are primarily indicated, as I have said, by the circus scenes. But, more intensely, they emerge in those moments when Lola is represented as thinking or reflecting. This happens quite often during the circus scenes, when the camera comes to focus closely on Lola and her face, where she will exhibit fatigue or pain, as though the weight of the past is pressing down upon her, causing her suffering and discontentment. This occurs early in the film, for example, when reenacting the wedding scene. Lola spins on a dais, and swoons, almost as though she will be unable to go on with the show. Such moments explicitly bring out the nature of so-called peaks of present. The past is here rising up so as to intersect with the present. In doing so, such peaks show us "a little time in the pure state," for this intersection of past and present is nothing other than a crystal-image.

For the film overall, the weight of the past, insofar as it pushes up against the present, is thematized by way of Lola's fragile heart. One of the plot points that recurs during the circus scenes pertains to Lola's medical condition. Lola often complains of being short of breath. Half-way through the film, her doctor (Carl Esmond) arrives at the circus tent so as to tell the circus manager (Friedrich Domin)—a manager who tends to his duties while dressed in a clown costume—that Lola suffers from a "weak heart." The implication is that she suffers from a physical condition, but the notion of a weak heart also refers to the trials and difficulties of Lola's love life. Her romantic attachments have always been cut short in one way or another, as with Franz Liszt, Claudio Pirotto, or, most affectingly, with King Ludwig. And her love affairs can be cut short by the sheer unsatisfactory nature of them, as occurs with her marriage to Lieutenant James. Lola's heart, in this sense, has certainly suffered and been made weak.

In the film's finale, Lola's trapeze act, the dramatization of her heart condition is given full force. As we already know, she has been advised against taking her final jump from on high without a net. The fear is that her heart will not be able to take the strain of the plunge. But this plunge is also a figure for her diving, once again, into her past. Lola's being raised up on high to the top of the tent, to the highest point of the trapeze contraption, is nothing less than her ascension to a "peak of present." And, as we shall see later, Ophuls's masterfully traces peaks of present and sheets of past in *Lola Montès* by way of traversals between high and low. Lola, having attained a peak of present high up on the trapeze, once again plunges into her past. She survives, and thus will again be destined to repeat these journeys into the past, night after night.

There are a range of scenes in which Ophuls plays with highs and lows, ups and downs, and, in doing so, accentuates the play between "peaks of present" and "sheets of past." In addition to the scenes in which Lola can be seen to be rising up to the trapeze platform in the circus, there are four main scenes in which up and down movements are accentuated: when Lola proposes to Lieutenant James at the Paris Opera; when staff at the King's palace need to find a needle and thread to mend Lola's dress; another when Lola and her entourage first look for rooms in Munich; and finally, the downward movement when Lola flees her own palace when revolution seems imminent. (One might also count the ringmaster's visit to Lola on the French Riviera. He ascends the stairs to meet her, then descends them to depart.) These scenes all feature a juxtapositions between high and low, with the highs typically evoking "peaks of present," while the lows take us in to "sheets of past." What each of these scenes dramatizes—noting that they are all flashbacks—is the play between the significance of an encounter in the present—a "peak of present"—and the encounter's significance as a "sheet of past." In short, they each evoke a splitting of time into past and present.

I shall deal in detail only with the first two of these scenes I have listed. The first of these scenes occurs when a sixteen-year-old Lola attends the Paris Opera with her mother. It is here that her mother intends to arrange for Lola to meet a somewhat elderly man—he is in his sixties—with the intention that Lola will be married to him. The action unfolds in a remarkable way. During the intermission of the opera performance, Lola and her mother, accompanied by Lieutenant James, for he has accompanied them on their journey from India to France, make their way to the entrance hall of the opera house. Above this foyer area is a range of balconies and staircases that enable access to the opera boxes. Thus, the camera follows the progress of the three characters as they enter the foyer area on the lower level. They then ascend to a raised balcony and walk across it, from right to left. Next, they ascend some stairs that lead to a second, higher balcony. They then walk across this from left to right. They again ascend to a higher level before crossing that from right to left. Eventually, and it is only here that we get the first edit of the scene, they reach the rooms where Lola may well be offered in marriage. The entire movement of the scene, up the stairs and across the balconies, is shot in a single take so that the camera moves and sways in accordance with the characters' movements. It is a quintessentially Ophulsian camera flourish.[59] In the room where they arrive, the meeting begins to take place. But, as we already know, Lola makes her escape. And thus we have the reverse action. Lola makes her way back down the balconies and staircases until she is once again at the bottom of the building's interior. Lieutenant James chases after her. When he catches up to her he declares that he will "do anything" for her. And so she proposes marriage.

The marriage proposal is depicted elaborately. We are still in a single take that has traced Lola's descent from on high. She now stands at a set of large, glass-paneled French doors that lead to an external courtyard. She asks for James's hand in marriage. Then she thrusts the doors open and runs into the courtyard. James follows her, deep into the far background of the shot, where a passionate kiss seals their intentions.

Where are the "peaks of present" and "sheets of past" here? The up and down movements dramatize the two approaches to time. On the one hand, we can see these events unfolding as a series of "peaks of present." Lola is confronted with a series of choices. In other words, she needs to make decisions "in the present." Can she bear to be married to the old man her mother wants her to marry? How can she get out of this predicament? She makes her escape. And then, "on the fly," as it were— that is, in the intensity of the moment, "in the present"—she proposes to Lieutenant James. All of these moments can be seen from the perspective of "peaks of present."

At the same time, however, the scene also delves into "sheets of past." As Deleuze puts it,

> What happens when we search for a recollection? We have to put ourselves into the past in general, then we have to choose between the regions: in which do we think that the recollection is hidden, huddled up waiting for us and evading us? . . . We have to jump into a chosen region, even if we have to return to the present to make another jump. (C2, 99)

What better way to characterize Lola's constant returns to the past in *Lola Montès*? In this particular scene, the sheets of past are themselves represented by levels of the balconies, as though giving material existence to Lola's attempts to jump into the various layers of her past, into her memories so as to fathom the significance of the choices she has made there, or the consequences of the events she has undergone. And we know that her decision to marry Lieutenant James was very much an escape from a worse fate: that of being married to a man old enough to be her grandfather. As the film progresses we will also come to know that her marriage to James ended badly, so that what was a positive choice from one perspective in the heat of a "peak of present" becomes a negative choice when seen from another perspective. This process of jumping into the past in order to survey and weigh up what happens there, to compare it with other "sheets" of past, is exactly what is at stake for Lola in this film.

Our second scene, one of the film's more famous scenes—and an evocation of an equally famous event in the life of the real Lola Montez—features Lola's first meeting with King Ludwig at his palace. Lola has been rejected by the Royal Theater after having auditioned for them. The King informs her that one reason for her rejection was because of her physique. "I've got a good figure," she declares, but the King informs her that, in fact, this was one of the problems. She therefore sets out to prove to Ludwig that her figure is indeed attractive. She rips open her dress to reveal the impressive nature of her bosom. And it is here that some members of the film's first audiences, apparently, were greatly disappointed. Their expectations of erotic display were quashed here, insofar as we see nothing that is at all scandalous. On the contrary, Ophuls cuts very rapidly to a doorway just outside the room where the King and Lola are conversing. Sitting just outside this door are two attendants who now appear to have been awoken from their slumber on account of a loud bell that has been rung. The bell has been rung by the King so as to summon these footmen to his chamber. A needle and thread will be needed to mend the dress that Lola has ripped. And so begins one of the film's most amusing routines.

The first footman, having received the request from the King, then passes on this request to the second footman. This footman then gets up and goes to a nearby doorway where he then tells yet another footman that a needle and thread are necessary. This footman then passes the message to yet another footman, and so on. Eventually one of these footmen then enters a central vestibule where, from up on high, he shouts down several floors below of the need for a needle and thread. There is thus an elaborate demonstration of the ways in which an entire small army of servants, maids, and butlers are all thrown into a frenzy over the request for a needle and thread. The items are ultimately gathered from the lowest depths of the palace, then taken back up the central staircases, thus completing the passage from high to low, then back to the heights where the necessary repairs are carried out.

Once again the up and down, high and low movements of the scene, mostly charted by the sort of mobile camera of which Ophuls was so fond, offers something akin to a graphical rendition of the relationship between the past and the present, of the ways in which the present recedes into layers of the past and of how the past rises up into "peaks" of the present. Most significant here is Lola's ability to act on the spur of the moment, for it is her "offer" made to the King here that lands her a role in the Theater—it is the "Royal" Theater after all, and the King's word carries substantial force there—as well as carrying her into the arms of the King. The up and down movements that chart the seeking of a needle and thread thus accentuate the layers of past that are also exhibited here: Lola's continuing search for the significance of what has happened to her and of the choices she has made, for the memories she has lost and of those she is attempting to renew.

The Spiritual Automaton

The dramatization of "peaks of present" and "sheets of past" provides an opening to another aspect of Deleuze *Cinema* books: the question of what it means to think. As we saw earlier, for Deleuze, thoughts are material. They do not exist "in the mind." They are connected to objects, matter, things in the world. Another point to consider is that, for Deleuze, thoughts are not necessarily under the control of a subject. They are not necessarily "my" thoughts in the sense of being under my control or my creations. For thought to operate, I must go outside myself. Thoughts, genuine thoughts, are things that come from outside the self.

If we consider the problem of thought from the perspective of the movement-image, then thoughts are most often connected with objects in the external world. A character perceives things, and a thought is thereby connected to and a consequence of what is seen. Typically, in films of the movement-image, a character will then act on the basis of this thought. Crucial to acknowledge here is that thought is connected with objects, with the objects perceived. A simple example (which I used earlier): if I am aiming to cross a road, then my thoughts will be connected with the objects I see before me. If I see cars coming along the road, I will not cross. If there are no cars approaching, I will cross. Thus, my thoughts are connected with, and cannot be separated from, the objects I encounter and the actions I will then perform. As we have seen at length, for the movement-image, perception leads to action and the perception-action circuit is motivated by need and utility.

Things are rather different for the time-image. Here, thoughts are associated with time. They are thus consequences of the way in which a character will be connected to the past and memory. But are not memories internal? Does not a journey into memory entail a journey to the deepest insides of myself? Therefore, how might it happen that, when confronted with thoughts that function in terms of the past and memory, such thoughts come from *outside* the subject? And furthermore, surely memories are immaterial: they are not composed of matter in the way that a stone, or a car, or a table is? Deleuze will counter such objections by stressing the material qualities of memories. And he also stresses that such memory thoughts can be said to originate outside the self. First of all, Deleuze considers that memories have a material quality. Suffice it to say that this is precisely what Bergson's *Matter and Memory* is about. He argues that memories are indeed made of matter, that thoughts are therefore "in" the world, and furthermore, that images are material. The images we form of things *are* those things and cannot be separated from them as though they might exist independently "in" our minds. All of this provides rich material for Deleuze's arguments in the *Cinema* books. Additionally, Proust's example of the petite madeleine, of the materiality of its texture when dipped into tea, or the liquid materiality of the tea itself: these are indicators of the materiality of memory.

We can see this emerging in the scenes from *Lola Montès* we have been discussing. The charting of movements from high to low, from peaks of present to sheets of past, is an attempt to render cinematically the materiality of the layers of the past and memory. When we encounter the layers of balconies at the opera house, or the interior levels of Ludwig's castle, Ophuls is attempting to evoke the material quality of the layers of pastness. But even more than this, the scenes evoke the sense that such memories are not produced by the self or subject. Rather, they have an existence outside the self. It is the task of the self to then go into or jump into those layers of the past. For the time-image, and for *Lola Montès*, such jumps are ones that go into pure memory: a jump into nonconscious memory, that is, layers of memory that are outside the self. Deleuze often makes remarks along these lines. He claims right near the end of *Cinema 2*, that "thought, as power which has not always existed, is born from an outside more distant than any external world, and, as power which does not yet exist, confronts an inside, an unthinkable or unthought, deeper than any internal world" (*C2*, 278).

I state all this as a way of reintroducing the notion of the "spiritual automaton." As we saw earlier, Deleuze adapts this term from the writings of Spinoza and makes it into a significant concept for the *Cinema* books. Spinoza's notion is one whose central quality is that ideas and thoughts are material. They do not simply exist "in" the mind. They exist as part of the material world. Thoughts and ideas are integrally related to and involved in the matter of the external world.

This additionally means, on Deleuze's reading of Spinoza, that thoughts are not produced by the self. They instead originate in the matter of the world which is external to the mind and external to the self. Therefore, the spiritual automaton is a way of defining the mechanism of thought or spirit. In other words, the kinds of immaterial notions typically associated with ideas and thoughts are here imbued with materiality. Thought is considered as a kind of machine, and the thoughts produced by the self are considered to be the products of an automaton. (A dictionary definition of automaton tells us that it is "a mechanical device operating under its own hidden power; e.g., a robot.") What this means for Deleuze is that thoughts can be considered as consequences of material production: a robotic, mechanized process. The "thinking thing" that characterizes human beings is not a disembodied soul in the manner envisaged by Descartes. Rather, the "thinking thing" is a machine, a spiritual automaton, composed of matter and intimately connected to the external world. The self or the subject is thus a *spiritual machine*, a mechanical contraption imbued with spirit.

For the time-image and *Lola Montès*, what is important to consider here is the relationship between the spiritual automaton and memory. What it means for our analysis is that Lola's jumping into the past, into memory, is akin to letting herself become automated, of letting the past and memory take hold of her so as to produce responses and thoughts in a machinic way. Another way to consider this is to conceive of Lola's memories as things that happen to her, rather than as things that are produced by her. This therefore provides us with the sense that Lola is passive in relation to those memories: she does not actively produce them. On the contrary, they produce her.

The Powers of the False

As a culmination and conclusion of our analysis of *Lola Montès*, I want to declare that Ophuls's film amounts to an exceptional example of what Deleuze, following Nietzsche, calls *the powers of the false*. One of the things that films of the time-image do is put the notion of truth into crisis. Where movement-image films provide narrations that produce truth, time-image films do not. As Deleuze puts it, narratives in films of the time-image give rise to "situations to which characters, who have become seers, cannot or will not react, so great is their need to 'see' properly what there is in the situation" (C2, 128). And we can immediately sense Lola's situation here. She is confronted with a life in the circus where she no longer knows how to act, respond, or react. All she can do is go back into her past, to see, to try to see properly, to fathom what there is of the situation in which she finds herself. It is out of such situations, out of a lack of ability to respond, that one will become a "man of dreams," as Bergson calls it, rather than a "man of action." This man of dreams—or woman, in the case of Lola—will no longer search for the true. Deleuze writes, "A new status of narration follows from this: narration ceases to be truthful, that is, to claim to be true, and becomes fundamentally falsifying." He goes on to then declare that "The images must be produced in such a way that the past is not necessarily true" (C2, 131). Such falsifying narration is central for *Lola Montès*. Primarily it is signaled by discrepancies between the circus reenactments of the past and those that are portrayed via flashback. So when the ringmaster declares that "Her [Lola's] happiness took root in the beautiful and generous soil of a happy family life," then we know the flashback does not give us anything like this. Rather, the flashback scenes of Lola with her mother are filled with disappointment and neglect, foregrounded in the scenes in which Lola and her mother travel by ship back from India to Europe. And much the same occurs when the ringmaster refers to Lola's "happy" marriage to Lieutenant James. Thus, on the one hand, we can declare that it is the flashbacks which falsify the circus scenes. But this would not be enough—that is, to declare the flashbacks true in a way that the circus scenes are false (and we have seen John Belton make such claims of *Lola Montès*). The narration of *Lola Montès* is, on the contrary, one in which we can no longer be certain if any of the reenactments or flashbacks are true. The whole of the film is guided, instead, by a principle of the powers of the false, a falsifying narration that undermines any and all claims to truth. This might be one way in which the film stays true (as it were) to the real Lola Montez, for the real Lola was adept at fabricating her life story, to the point of changing her name, her family, her country of origin, or embarking on at least three marriages (even though the annulment of her first marriage rendered such subsequent ventures illegal), and much more besides. And we also know that, during her later years—in her thirties—she often wrote and performed in dramatizations of her own life, so that the sense in which the life of the "real" Lola Montez was always already a fabrication—a falsification—is central to the life and history of Lola. That Ophuls's film of *Lola Montès* remains faithful to the falsifying history of Lola Montez is appropriate, to say the least.[60]

Integral to the notion of the powers of the false is that it undermines what Deleuze refers to as the "system of judgment." What does a judge do? He decrees what is true and what is false. On this basis he can then also separate good from evil. Deleuze goes so far as to decree that the form of the true, and of separating good from evil, is central to films of the movement-image. We can see as much in a film like *La signora di tutti*. Gaby's quest to separate true and good acts from false ones has deeply negative consequences in Gaby's suicide. At the end of the film we know her relationship with Leonardo has been fatal—it has been false—while her love for Roberto had been good and true. (We may even come to judge her relationship with Leonardo as a kind of evil, especially as it entailed a deception of Leonardo's wife, Alma.) And so too are such divisions integral for *Letter from an Unknown Woman*. Lisa's true love for Stefan is demonstrated to have been true and good in the sense that it delivered to Lisa the happiest moments of her life. Her other relationships, with the Lieutenant in Linz, with her husband, Johan Stauffer, and even her relationship with her mother, are all deemed false from the perspective of the heights of the true she experienced with Stefan. True is clearly distinguished from false.

Time-image films do not function in such a way. They do away with the system of judgment. We can see this quite definitively in Ophuls's magnificent *La Ronde*. There, relationships are just relationships. They happen and that is that. No system of judgment is deployed to tell us that one kind of relationship is better than another, for example, that the love and lust exhibited by a married couple is superior to that experienced by a soldier and a prostitute. On the contrary, no such comparisons between good and evil, or true and false, are involved. The question of the true is simply no longer an issue. It is in this way that what Deleuze calls the powers of the false takes hold.

Does this therefore mean we are destined to live in a false world? Is that what Deleuze means? Does it mean that nihilism has triumphed and we now must simply praise falsehood and forego the true? No, not at all. What Deleuze means to argue is that we should never simply accept the true as true. Rather, we must ceaselessly question any so-called truth so as to subject it to scrutiny. Whatever truth there is can always be improved to become a better kind of truth. But in order for a better truth to be born, the existing truth must be rendered false. This is what time-image films and the powers of the false aspire to: crushing the true so that, eventually, in another age, in the future, a new and better true might be born.

Deleuze phrases these arguments in some of the most captivating moments of *Cinema 2*. His arguments here hinge on articulating what he calls "belief in this world." At issue in Deleuze's claims here is the conviction that today—and, in general, by "today" he means the years following the Second World War and into the present, when the time-image emerged—we have ceased to believe in the world. Now we merely accept what we are told about the world. We accept what tradition and elders—our teachers, our masters—tell us to believe. We believe all this without genuinely reckoning whether those truths about the world may have any validity. We "pretend to believe."

We can see how this attitude of "pretending to believe" takes hold in *Lola Montès*. The ringmaster gives Lola directions, he puts words in her mouth, he tells her where to walk and dance, to smoke a particular brand of cigar, and he retells the events of her life. The ringmaster, to this degree, tells the "truth." He imposes a truth on Lola's history and life. And then, it is by way of the flashback scenes that Lola then comes to question to kinds of truths posed by the ringmaster. The flashbacks falsify the ringmaster's claims. In doing so, Lola tries to reinvent her past, to undermine the truths that have been asserted about her past. Thus, she tries to establish some level of belief in those events and their consequences. This does not mean that, by the end of the film, Lola establishes a new "truth" of her life, or even a new belief in the world. I have stressed throughout that Lola's role is passive, whether we see that as being governed by what Spinoza calls "passive affections," or by Deleuze's "passive syntheses of time." Lola is primarily passive. We might also see Lola's situation as one governed by what Nietzsche calls "reactive forces." Much of the challenge of *Lola Montès* is to chart the ways in which Lola resists conceding to reactive forces. To fully concede to such forces would lead only to *ressentiment* and nihilism. On the contrary, Lola draws upon her reserves of strength and challenges the so-called truths of her past. She jumps back into her past to see what she will find there. Her quest is to potentially reinvent that past in ways that will restore her belief in this world.

I claimed earlier that Lisa, in *Letter from an Unknown Woman*, achieves the Nietzschean goal of "becoming who she is." *Letter* presents us with a definitive expression of Lisa's life, of her determination that her love for Stefan was worth it, and that it delivered happiness for her. In short, it is by virtue of her love that Lisa was able to "become who she is." We can call this the truth of her life, an expression of her discovery of a "true" and a "good" by which to define her life.

Letter from an Unknown Woman is, as I have argued, a movement-image film. The stakes for *Lola Montès*, a time-image film, are considerably different. Does Lola "become who she is" in *Lola Montès*? The answer can only be no, especially if we consider the film's ending. Lola, contained within a cage, can scarcely deliver an image of triumphant satisfaction or happiness. But that is much the point of *Lola Montès* and of the time-image more generally. The battles of life are never easily won, and easily won victories may typically turn out to be only victories in disguise. Thus, it is always worth reconsidering one's situation. It is worth going back into the past, into one's memories, to see what one will find there. To revisit one's past and to reinvent one's past is perhaps the chief aim of films of the time-image. As we have already seen Deleuze say, "The images [in films of the time-image] must be produced in such a way that the past is not necessarily true" (*C2*, 131). And even though Lola does not "become who she is," she attains what might be an even more admirable position: that of an ongoing becoming. The notion of becoming, an ongoing becoming, is central to *Lola Montès*, for "becoming is the power of the false," writes Deleuze (*C2*, 142). "And it is clear," he adds, "that becoming is always innocent, even in crime, even in the exhausted life in so far as it is still a becoming" (*C2*, 142). And so, tomorrow night Lola will return, once again, exhausted, sick, and struggling, to continue the task of becoming who she is.

NOTES

Chapter 1

1 J.-L. Baudry, "Ideological Effects of the Basic Cinematographic Apparatus," in B. Nichols (Ed.), *Movies and Methods Volume II* (Berkeley, Los Angeles, and London: University of California Press, 1985), pp. 531–42; G. Debord, *The Society of the Spectacle*, trans. D. Nicholson-Smith (New York: Zone Books, 1994); T. Adorno and M. Horkheimer, *Dialectic of Enlightenment*, trans. J. Cumming (London: Allen Lane, 1973). See also, D.N. Rodowick, *The Crisis of Political Modernism: Criticism and Ideology in Contemporary Film Theory*, 2nd Edition (Urbana: University of Illinois Press, 1994).

2 For an excellent account of this aspect of Hollywood cinema, see David Bordwell, *Reinventing Hollywood: How 1940s Filmmakers Changed Movie Storytelling* (Chicago, IL: University of Chicago Press, 2017).

3 François Furet, *Interpreting the French Revolution*, trans. Elborg Foster (Cambridge: Cambridge University Press, 1981).

4 Gilles Deleuze, *Foucault*, trans. Seán Hand (London: Athlone, 1988).

5 Michel Foucault, *History of Madness*, trans. Jean Khalfa (London: Routledge, 2006).

6 Michel Foucault, *Discipline and Punish: The Birth of the Prison*, trans. Alan Sheridan (London: Allen Lane, 1977).

7 Friedrich Nietzsche, *Thus Spoke Zarathustra: A Book for All and None*, in *The Portable Nietzsche*, trans. and ed. by Walter Kaufmann (New York: Viking Press, 1954), p. 351.

8 Friedrich Nietzsche, *The Gay Science*, trans. Walter Kaufmann (New York: Vintage, 1974), p. 219 (§270).

9 Friedrich Nietzsche, *Ecce Homo: How One Becomes What One Is*, in *Basic Writings of Nietzsche*, trans. and ed. by Walter Kaufmann (New York: The Modern Library, 1968), p. 657.

10 Friedrich Nietzsche, *On the Genealogy of Morality*, trans. Carol Diethe (Cambridge: Cambridge University Press, 1994), p. 3.

11 Gilles Deleuze, *Nietzsche and Philosophy*, trans. Hugh Tomlinson (London: Athlone, 1983), Section 2, pp. 39–72.

12 Nietzsche, *Genealogy*, p. 8.

13 Deleuze, *Nietzsche and Philosophy*, p. 66.

14 Ibid.

15 Michel Foucault, "Nietzsche, Genealogy, History," in D.F. Bouchard (Ed.), *Language, Counter-Memory, Practice: Selected Essays and Interviews* (Ithaca, NY: Cornell University Press, 1977), p. 152.

16 Friedrich Nietzsche, "On the Uses and Disadvantages of History for Life," trans. R.J. Hollingdale (Cambridge: Cambridge University Press, 1997), p. 75.

17 On these points, see Robert B. Pippin, *Nietzsche, Psychology, and First Philosophy* (Chicago: University of Chicago Press, 2010), pp. 100–1.

18 On this point, see D.N. Rodowick, *Gilles Deleuze's Time Machine* (Durham: Duke University Press, 1997), p. 18.

19 Keith Ansell Pearson, *Philosophy and the Adventure of the Virtual: Bergson and the Time of Life* (London: Routledge, 2002), p. 78.

20 Gilles Deleuze, *Expressionism in Philosophy: Spinoza*, trans. Martin Joughin (New York: Zone Books, 1992), p. 218.

21 Baruch Spinoza, *Ethics*, trans. Andrew Boyle (London: Everyman, 1993), p. 197 (V.3).

22 On all of these points see Deleuze, *Expressionism*, p. 140, 153.

23 Deleuze, *Expressionism*, pp. 283–4.

24 Baudry, "Ideological Effects," p. 535.

25 I make this argument in Rushton, *The Reality of Film: Theories of Filmic Reality* (Manchester: Manchester University Press, 2011), Chapter 5, pp. 126–47.

26 Tag Gallagher in his commentary on the UK release DVD of *Letter from an Unknown Woman*. Released by Second Sight, 2006.

27 Tag Gallagher on the DVD commentary.

28 See Tania Modleski, "Time and Desire in the Woman's Film," *Cinema Journal* 23, no. 3 (1984), pp. 19–30.

29 Gaylyn Studlar, "Masochistic Performance and Female Subjectivity in *Letter from an Unknown Woman*," *Cinema Journal* 33, no. 3 (1995), p. 48.

NOTES 179

30 Gilles Deleuze, *Coldness and Cruelty*, trans. Jean McNeil, in
Masochism, New York: Zone Books, 1991, pp. 32–3.
31 Ibid., p. 71.
32 Studlar, "Masochistic Performance," p. 50.
33 George M. Wilson, *Narration in Light: Studies in Cinematic Point
of View* (Baltimore: Johns Hopkins University Press, 1986), p. 107.
34 Ibid., p. 120.
35 Ibid.
36 See Stanley Cavell, *Cities of Words: Pedagogical Letters on a
Register of the Moral Life* (Cambridge, MA: Harvard University
Press, 2004), p. 389.
37 See Stanley Cavell, *Contesting Tears: The Hollywood
Melodrama of the Unknown Woman* (Chicago and London:
University of Chicago Press, 1996), p. 107; Cavell, *Cities of
Words*, p. 407.
38 Cavell, *Cities of Words*, p. 407.
39 Nietzsche, *On the Genealogy of Morality*, p. 3.
40 Deleuze, *Coldness and Cruelty*, pp. 32–3.
41 See Gilles Deleuze and Félix Guattari, *A Thousand Plateaus:
Capitalism and Schizophrenia*, trans. Brian Massumi (Minnesota:
University of Minnesota Press, 1987), pp. 192–207; Gilles
Deleuze, "On the Superiority of Anglo-American Literature," in
Dialogues II (New York: Continuum, 2002), pp. 36–76.
42 Deleuze, "On the Superiority," p. 36.
43 D.H. Lawrence, *Studies in Classic American Literature*
(Harmondsworth: Penguin, 1971), p. 142; quoted in Ronald
Bogue, *Deleuze on Literature* (New York: Routledge, 2003), p.
152. See also Deleuze, "On the Superiority," p. 36.
44 V.F. Perkins, "*Letter from an Unknown Woman*," *Movie: A
Journal of Film Criticism* (online), no. 7 (2017), p. 87. (Article
originally published in *Movie* 29–30, 1982.)
45 Ophuls's film is an adaptation of a short story written by Stefan
Zweig. The story is reprinted, along with the Shooting Script
of the film, in *Letter from an Unknown Woman: Max Ophuls,
Director*, ed. Virginia Wright Wexman (New Brunswick, NJ:
Rutgers University Press, 1986).
46 Nietzsche, *The Gay Science*, p. 274 (§341).
47 See Edward Branigan, *Narrative Comprehension and Film*
(London: Routledge, 1992), pp. 177–91. I discuss some aspects
on Branigan's writing here in relation to Deleuze in Rushton,

"Passions and Actions: Deleuze's Cinematographic Cogito,"
Deleuze Studies 2, no. 2 (2008), pp. 121–39.

48 For an account of these aspects of the "action-image" in
Deleuze's writings, see Rushton, *Cinema After Deleuze*
(London: Continuum, 2012), especially chapters 3 and 4, pp.
27–57.

49 Branigan, *Narrative Comprehension*, pp. 184–9.

50 On these points in relation to the visual arts, also see Gilles
Deleuze, *Francis Bacon: The Logic of Sensation*, trans. Daniel W.
Smith (London: Continuum, 2003).

51 Deleuze also discusses the notion of the "Dividual" in relation to
Eisenstein's montages; *C1*, 92.

52 See Béla Balázs, "The Close-Up," and "The Face of Man," in
Theory of the Film (New York: Arno Press, 1972), pp. 52–88; and
Jean Epstein, "Magnification," and "On Certain Characteristics
of *Photogénie*," in Richard Abel (Ed.), *French Film Theory
and Criticism, A History / Anthology, Volume 1: 1907–1929*
(Princeton, NJ: Princeton University Press, 1988), pp. 235–42,
314–18.

53 Perkins, "*Letter*," p. 87.

54 On Deleuze's distinction between "reflective" and "intensive"
faces, see Rushton, "What Can a Face Do? On Deleuze and
Faces," *Cultural Critique* 51 (2002), pp. 219–37.

55 Cavell makes a great deal of these words in his reading of the
film. See Cavell, *Cities of Words*, pp. 396–7.

56 Wilson, *Narration in Light*, p. 124.

57 Laura Mulvey, "Love, History, and Max Ophuls: Repetition
and Difference in Three Films of Doomed Romance," *Film and
History: An Interdisciplinary Journal* 43, no. 1 (2013), p. 28.

58 Wilson, *Narration in Light*, p. 123.

59 Ibid., p. 124.

Chapter 2

1 Such is the way Deleuze formulates this process in relation to the
great flashback films of Joseph Mankiewicz—*A Letter to Three
Wives* (1949), *All About Eve* (1950), and *The Barefoot Contessa*
(1954). See *Cinema 2*, p. 52.

2 Gilles Deleuze, "The Actual and the Virtual," in *Dialogues II* (London: Continuum, 2006), p. 150.

3 Ibid., p. 148.

4 See Rushton, *Cinema After Deleuze*, pp. 27–40; and *C1*, 141–59.

5 Henri Bergson, "Memory and False Recognition," in *Bergson: Key Writings* (London: Continuum, 2002), pp. 148–9.

6 See John Mullarkey, *Bergson and Philosophy* (Edinburgh: Edinburgh University Press, 1999), p. 49.

7 I prefer "nonconscious" to the "unconscious" Bergson favors. For a long and detailed account of Bergson and the "unconscious," see Gilles Deleuze, *Bergsonism* (New York: Zone Books, 1991), pp. 56–72.

8 See Henri Bergson, *Matière et Mémoire: Essai sur la relation du corps a l'esprit* (Paris: Félix Alcan, 1928), p. 167.

9 Bruce Seymour, *Lola Montez: A Life* (New Haven, CT: Yale University Press, 2009), p. 297. I have relied on Seymour's biography for an account of the "real" Lola Montez.

10 Martina Müller, "The Making of Max Ophuls' *Lola Montès / Lola Montez*," *Arizona Quarterly* 60, no. 5 (2004), p. 26.

11 Ibid., 34.

12 François Truffaut, "*Lola Montès*," in *The Films in My Life* (New York: Simon & Schuster, 1978), p. 229.

13 Andrew Sarris, "Films in Focus," *The Village Voice*, September 5, 1963, p. 9.

14 Deleuze, "The Actual and the Virtual," p. 148.

15 Seymour, *Lola Montez*, p. 54.

16 Ronald Bogue, *Deleuze on Cinema* (London: Routledge, 2003), p. 121.

17 Ibid., pp. 121–2.

18 In her DVD commentary on the UK release of *Lola Montès* by Second Sight (2008).

19 Gilles Deleuze, *Difference and Repetition*, trans. Paul Patton (London: Athlone, 1994), p. 208. This passage is italicized in the original.

20 Ibid., p. 209.

21 Deleuze, "The Actual and the Virtual," p. 148.

22 John Belton, "The Commodification of Romanticism," *Camera Obscura* 30, no. 3 (2015), p. 5.

23 Deleuze, *Difference and Repetition*, p. 211.

24 Deleuze, *Bergsonism*, pp. 91–113.

25 Deleuze, "The Actual and the Virtual," p. 151.

26 Immanuel Kant, *Inaugural Dissertation (On the Form and Principles of the Sensible and the Intelligible World)*, in *Theoretical Philosophy, 1955–1770*, ed. David Walford (Cambridge: Cambridge University Press, 1992), p. 395 (§14).

27 Immanuel Kant, *Critique of Pure Reason*, trans. Norman Kemp Smith (London: Macmillan, 1929), p. 74; A30/B46.

28 Ibid., p. 77; A34/B50.

29 Gilles Deleuze, "On Four Poetic Formulas That Might Summarize the Kantian Philosophy," in *Essays Critical and Clinical*, trans. Daniel W. Smith (London: Verso, 1998), pp. 27–35.

30 Marcel Proust, *Swann's Way, In Search of Lost Time, Volume 1*, trans. C.K.S. Moncreiff and T. Kilmartin (London: Chatto & Windus, 1981), p. 60.

31 Gilles Deleuze, *Proust and Signs: The Complete Text*, trans. Richard Howard (London: Athlone, 2000), p. 37. See also Deleuze, *Difference and Repetition*, p. 85.

32 Deleuze, "On Four Poetic Formulas," p. 29.

33 Ibid., 31.

34 Ibid.

35 Laura Mulvey, "Visual Pleasure and Narrative Cinema," *Screen* 16, no. 3 (1975), pp. 6–18.

36 Laura Mulvey, "Compulsion to Repeat: Max Ophuls' *Lola Montès*," *Afterall* 35, (2014), p. 91.

37 Susan White, *The Cinema of Max Ophuls: Magisterial Vision and the Figure of Woman* (New York: Columbia University Press, 1995), pp. 261ff.

38 Belton, "The Commodification of Romanticism," p. 11.

39 Mulvey, "Compulsion to Repeat," p. 93.

40 Belton, "The Commodification of Romanticism," p. 21.

41 Belton qualifies his claims. "*Lola Montès* is a film about spectacle. It is both a spectacle and a critique of spectacle . . . . Rather than seeing *Lola Montès* as only a denunciation of spectacle, I want to suggest that it remains somewhat ambivalent about it." "The Commodification of Romanticism," p. 14.

42 White, *The Cinema of Max Ophuls*, p. 274.

43 See Ibid., p. 294.

44 On this point, see Gilles Deleuze, "The Simulacrum and Ancient Philosophy," in *The Logic of Sense*, trans. Mark Lester (New York: Columbia University Press, 1990), pp. 253–79.

45 Belton, "The Commodification of Romanticism," p. 11.
46 A similar point is made in Alan Williams, *Max Ophuls and the Cinema of Desire: Style and Spectacle in Four Films, 1948–55* (New York: Arno Press, 1980), p. 150.
47 Belton, "The Commodification of Romanticism," p. 5.
48 Kaja Silverman, *The Subject of Semiotics* (New York: Oxford University Press, 1983), p. 228.
49 Spinoza, *Ethics* V.3, p. 197.
50 Deleuze, *Expressionism in Philosophy*, p. 284.
51 On this point see Rushton, *Cinema After Deleuze*, pp. 101–17.
52 Deleuze, *Difference and Repetition*, p. 70.
53 Ibid., p. 76.
54 Ibid., p. 71.
55 Ibid., p. 73.
56 Ibid., p. 75.
57 Ibid., p. 90. Also see Daniela Voss, "Deleuze's Third Synthesis of Time," *Deleuze Studies* 7, no. 2 (2013), pp. 194–216.
58 My interpretation of these issues differs greatly from that of Patricia Pisters's account in *The Neuro-Image: A Deleuzian Film-Philosophy of Digital Screen Culture* (Stanford, CA: Stanford University Press, 2012). Also see Rushton, "Passions and Actions."
59 On Ophuls's camera movements see Daniel Morgan, "Max Ophuls and the Limits of Virtuosity: On the Aesthetics and Ethics of Camera Movement," *Critical Inquiry* 38, no. 1 (2011), pp. 127–63.
60 The real Lola Montez published a book of beauty tips, *The Arts of Beauty, or, Secrets of a Lady's Toilet* (New York: Dick & Fitzgerald, 1858), while her lectures and autobiography are also published as *Lectures of Lola Montez, Including her Biography*, Ed. C.C. Burr (New York: Rudd & Carleton, 1858).

INDEX